Change Your Life, and Keep the Change

Harnessing the Power
of Your Unconscious Mind
to Effortlessly Change Your Life

Change Your Life, and Keep the Change

Harnessing the Power
of Your Unconscious Mind
to Effortlessly Change Your Life

Gary Dooley

BOOKS

Winchester, UK
Washington, USA

First published by O-Books, 2011
O-Books is an imprint of John Hunt Publishing Ltd., Laurel House, Station Approach,
Alresford, Hants, SO24 9JH, UK
office1@o-books.net
www.o-books.com

For distributor details and how to order please visit the 'Ordering' section on our website.

ISBN: 978 1 84694 832 9

A CIP catalogue record for this book is available from the British Library.

Design: Lee Nash

Printed in the UK by CPI Antony Rowe
Printed in the USA by Offset Paperback Mfrs, Inc

We operate a distinctive and ethical publishing philosophy in all
areas of our business, from our global network of authors to
production and worldwide distribution.

CONTENTS

Introduction

This book will show you how to use your unconscious mind to create and sustain high self-esteem and greater self-confidence – effortlessly. Since we're unaware of everything we unconsciously do, any changes we make at an unconscious level must by definition require no effort on our part to sustain. This is the principle of least effort: the idea that we can achieve more by doing less and once we understand how it works we can learn how to do nothing yet achieve everything.

Surely this is too good to be true! How can we create emotional change without any effort? How can we get what we want without trying?

We're already doing it.

Think about this from the opposite perspective for a moment. Would it be possible to get what we *don't* want without any effort? Could we create fear, worry, anxiety, panic attacks or a state of depression without trying? Of course we could. People all over the world are doing it right now.

How much conscious effort do you think people make to create and sustain the feelings of low self-esteem or lack of self-confidence? How hard do they have to work to cultivate and maintain a debilitating sense of anxiety and fear? Do these restrictive emotions flow effortlessly into their lives or are they the product of hard conscious effort requiring 100% commitment and the full focus of their attention 24/7?

We already know the answer to these questions, yet we seem to have forgotten that this is a two-way street. What flows effortlessly one way must flow as effortlessly the other way, as long as we understand how to redirect the subconscious traffic.

No one would torture themselves with a panic attack or intentionally keep themselves stuck in the self-restricting trance of unworthiness we call low self-esteem. These negative emotional experiences are not the result of a conscious desire to be unhappy; they are the legacy of something that is happening unconsciously – something we're totally unaware of. This poses something of a challenge: how can we ever hope to change what we are doing if we don't know we're doing it?

In the pages that follow we'll find out. We'll learn how our unconscious mind influences every aspect of our life, how we've programmed it to do what it does, and how it can be re-programmed to create positive emotional change.

The unconscious mind may be both the least understood and most written-about aspect of humankind. No one understands it completely – even the 'experts' in the field remain divided in their opinions. At the end of the 19th century Dr Sigmund Freud, an Austrian neurologist, began to develop his theories on the unconscious mind and the powerful impact it has on our lives. We often assume he coined the term 'subconscious', but in fact the innovative American psychologist William James had been using it for years and mentions it in his 1890 book *Principles of Psychology*. Freud believed that we are driven subconsciously and that everything we do stems from a powerful yet subconscious desire to avoid pain or pursue pleasure. While this theory may seem logical, his close contemporary Dr Carl Jung, a pioneering Swiss psychiatrist, suspected that there was far more to human beings than thissubconscious pain/pleasure trigger.. Jung is the founder of analytical psychology, whose core principle is that we all have a deep subconscious desire to find meaning in our lives, to seek a sense of self and purpose. He referred to this cathartic search as 'individuation', a psychological journey of change, resulting in the discovery of our true self and the greater purpose of our life.

Almost every religion in the world holds the same principle as a core value of its teaching. Hinduism, Christianity, Islam, Buddhism and Taoism all maintain that we're more than the sum of our physical body and that life has a spiritual purpose. Jung spent much of his life developing his ideas, and many continue to be evident in therapeutic contexts today, such as the concepts of archetypes, synchronicity, and the principle of collective consciousness. The subject of our subconscious mind continues to fuel speculation because it remains an area of great mystery and amazement. We still don't fully know what it is capable of achieving.

This is a book anyone can use without the need for any prior knowledge of the unconscious mind. It is a simple book because change is best created through simplicity and the path of least resistance. It will teach you how to empower your unconscious mind in support of any lifestyle change you choose, though our goal will remain one of unconscious confidence and higher self-esteem. (Throughout, I have used the word 'unconscious' in preference to 'subconscious', because the prefix *sub-* may be interpreted to indicate something of less importance, and the unconscious is at least as important as the conscious.) Each chapter appears in an order designed to offer maximum benefit, so I suggest taking each as it comes, progressing to the next in your own time and at your convenience.

The content is based on the successful Life Balance Personal Development Course and includes relevant exercises to support your unconscious change. These are a helpful resource as you make progress, yet we all have different needs and requirements, therefore use only those exercises that are effective, and disregard any that prove otherwise. Under no circumstances should you continue with an exercise that causes any unpleasant side effects, though this is highly unlikely to happen if the exercises are used as described.

You will also find a number of stories which may prove useful. People have been telling stories for thousands of years; in fact there are probably no new stories in the world, just old ones with a new slant. Accept the stories you find here in that spirit. None of them belong to me, but since stories tend to change a little over time with each new telling, they inevitably carry my own slant. Take whatever you will from each of them; after all, they have no meaning other than the one you may attribute.

This book explores how we unconsciously do what we do and how we can alter that subliminal conditioning in a sustainable and positive way.Let me make it clear at the outset that I do not suggest the conscious mind is unproductive or of less importance than the unconscious; clearly they are both essential to our well-being and vital to our survival. Consciousness is actually our most productive resource, for in that state of pure awareness it is impossible to sustain the self-destructive illusions of low self-esteem.

Also, as you journey through these pages, please try to resist any temptation to label your unconscious mind as good or bad, for in truth it acts with detached indifference to the subliminal programming it receives. It is neither good nor bad but simply is. Blaming our unconscious mind for the negative emotions it initiates is like blaming our phone for the bad news it gives us. Milton H. Erickson, a 20th century American psychiatrist, believed our unconscious mind held the solution to every emotional problem, and most of the evidence suggests he was right. So what should we believe – that everything our unconscious mind does comes from our subliminal need to seek pleasure or avoid pain, as Freud suggested? Or shall we believe, with Jung, that something else is involved: an unconscious desire for a sense of spirituality and purpose in our lives?

The journey to unconscious confidence begins here, though the pathway will take us through an amazing and informative landscape. We begin in search of self-esteem: the true appreciation of who we really are behind the social mask we show to the world. Is this search no more than a desire to create a shift in self-perception or is it the first step in the journey of personal awareness? Is our unconscious mind just an extremely effective biological computer that runs any program we load with detached impartiality, or is it an enigmatic source of wisdom and strength?

If Jung and Erickson were right, there may be far more to us than most of us realize. If our unconscious mind holds the answers to some of the most important questions we could ask, we may have some extremely interesting personal discoveries waiting for us on the journey that lies ahead.

Gary Dooley
July 2010

1

Unconsciously Unstoppable

1

Mind is the forerunner of all things.
Buddha

I watched with fascination as my daughter leaned first one way then the other, turning the remote control in her hands as if it were the steering wheel of a car. I'd done the same just moments before as I negotiated the 'streets' of Florence. We both knew at a conscious level that we were playing a computerized racing game and it was the buttons on the remote control that made the cars turn (we had chosen not to connect a steering wheel accessory). We knew that tilting our arms would not influence the direction of the vehicles on the screen. Why then were we turning our arms in an attempt to steer?

We've all seen similar examples: players leaning one way or another in a futile attempt to coax the direction of a bowling ball after it has left their hand; passengers in a car unconsciously applying their foot to an invisible brake; a football coach trying to steer the ball as it flies towards a goal 50 yards away.

Why would anyone try to influence something that they realize is beyond their physical control? It seems insanely optimistic, even ridiculous, yet we all do it – for a very simple reason.

Our unconscious mind is easily seduced by interesting and compelling images. If we become totally engrossed in watching something, we may enter a light state of mindlessness – a kind of trance. As our consciousness starts to diminish, the part of our mind that controls our physical responses believes what it can see, and reacts accordingly.

In this chapter we will explore the potential of our unconscious mind, how it affects every aspect of our lives, our emotional state and, not least, the quality of our self-esteem. Our unconscious mind may be the most powerful and amazing resource we have, yet the most mysterious and underused. Although it is an essential key for personal change of any kind, most of us completely ignore it when we need it most. It seems we will look anywhere, consider anything, and speak to anyone in our efforts to change, while completely ignoring the wealth of untapped potential that lies within our own mind.

Dr Milton Erickson, founder president of the American Society for Clinical Hypnosis and a primary influence in the development of Neuro-Linguistic Programming, believed the unconscious mind was the most intelligent resource we have at our disposal, capable of resolving any emotional issue. He gained a reputation for helping people to quickly overcome a wide range of psychological problems; clients who'd been in expensive therapy programs for years without much success would often resolve their issues after just a few sessions with him. The secret of Erickson's success seemed to lie in his understanding that we all have the potential to self-heal and create any emotional change we desire *if* we know how to tap into the formidable power of our unconscious mind.

Once one knows the secrets of the mind, one will uncover the nature of all realities. By knowing the one, one will know all. This is the nature of the mind.
Tibetan saying

If Erickson was right, why do people continue to suffer from a wide range of psychological and emotional issues? If our unconscious mind is so smart, why doesn't it simply fix our emotional problems as soon as they show up?

7

Bill O'Hanlon, author of more than 30 books and one-time student of Erickson, offers us his own take on this subject: 'The unconscious mind is smart about what it's smart about, it's dumb about what it's dumb about, and smart about things it's dumb to be smart about.'

Confused?

You're entitled to be, but take comfort from the fact that there isn't a person alive who knows exactly how our unconscious mind works. Though we're living in relatively enlightened times, we are only now starting to scratch the surface of this fascinating subject. However, we're by no means entirely in the dark. We know, for example, that the unconscious mind has an almost infinite capacity to store memories, to organize and catalogue any unresolved traumatic experiences and emotions, and then to re-release them, seemingly without any logical reasoning. We also know it operates at lightning speeds and regards every experience as real – a fact that can work powerfully for or against us, providing us with a powerful asset in the process of change.

Many people speak about this aspect of their mind as though it is located somewhere in the brain, but of course there's no such thing in hard physical terms as a subconscious. It isn't something that can be sent off to the lab to be analyzed like a roll of film or a sample of blood. Thousands of autopsies have taken place in which a brain is removed and dissected, but no one has ever found a subconscious or an unconscious mind. When we refer to the subconscious mind we're speaking metaphorically to describe a process rather than an item.

The unconscious mind is a real enigma. Although its power seems almost infinite, and it can be utilized to create any change we desire, we must acknowledge that it isn't who *we are* and it certainly isn't infallible in its choice of strategy. The unconscious mind is programmed to keep us safe yet in doing so may initiate strategies which have unpleasant side effects.

For example, a friend recently confessed to me that he had never been outside Europe due to his fear of flying. 'I don't do planes,' he half-joked. This confident, self-assured man is instantly paralyzed with fear at the thought of boarding an aircraft, yet his fear isn't generated consciously since he wouldn't intentionally do this to himself; it's a result of something that is taking place unconsciously. But what kind of underlying intention drives his unconscious mind to induce this fear-based drama? Does it derive pleasure from tormenting him, like an evil demon might? Or is it more likely that this fear is the legacy of an unconscious desire to protect the system from a perceived threat to its well-being?

The unconscious mind is neither good nor evil; it simply is, and responds obediently to the programming we introduce. If we condition it to associate death and carnage with air travel, it won't respond by arguing a case against the potential for self-destruction; it will simply do what it's hard-wired to do: initiate the emotional reaction most likely to keep us away from airplanes. Such a strategy keeps my friend safe, though with the unpleasant side effect of paralyzing fear. Happily, a fear of flying, or of anything else, can be permanently removed by simply rewriting the appropriate programs of the unconscious mind.

The whole idea of unconscious re-programming may sound slightly abstract – how do we re-program something that no one has ever seen, that has no specific location in the brain? Don't worry – you don't have to completely understand how unconscious re-programming works in order to use it to produce the change you seek, just as we don't need to understand electricity to get light. If it seems unrealistic to believe your mind already holds all the solutions you'll ever need, imagine how unrealistic it was 200 years ago to believe we could walk into a room, flick on a switch, and in a split second produce light.

You don't get to choose how you're going to die ... you only get to choose how you're going to live.
Joan Baez

I have no idea how the internal combustion engine works, but this doesn't stop me driving to work every day. Likewise, if we want to create lasting change in our life, we need only remain open-minded and apply the skills we will learn here to find evidence of the potential we hold in our mind. Since our unconscious mind influences us whether we understand how it works or not, the choice is either to dismiss this fact, or learn to harness its power to help us achieve our goals.

Science is now beginning to understand the potential of the human mind; ideas that were regarded as nonsense 50 years ago are being taken seriously by researchers. Noetic science, for example, is the study of how our mind provides guidance and how we instinctively know if something is good or bad for our well-being. This form of non-rational knowing is a natural resource we all access at times. We don't know how or why we know something isn't quite right; we just sense it and react accordingly.

Noetic science was once the domain of a few innovative and open-minded researchers but is now rapidly raising its profile in public awareness. The idea that people intuitively 'know' things is not new, however; some of the world's oldest cultures have known this for centuries. 'Noetic' is derived from the Greek word *nous*, a term widely used today to imply clear understanding. 'Noesis' means insight, and noetic researchers have discovered we all have a natural ability to access our personal insight, even though we usually ignore it – with regrettable consequences.

This intuitive guidance doesn't manifest itself through the internal voice in our head; it shows up as a feeling around the area of our abdomen, hence the expression 'gut feeling'. It appears without any conscious effort, as if something beyond our awareness is trying to provide help and guidance when we need it most.

At an unconscious level, we are capable of computing and assessing billions of incoming data combinations in a split second, which explains why we can unconsciously evaluate the potential risk-factor in any situation. The conscious results of these split-second subliminal assessments then show up around the gut area. If we learn to recognize and trust this natural source of intuitive guidance, instead of listening to the voice in our head, we may save ourselves a lot of avoidable unhappiness.

Some of the greatest thinkers in history understood how to tune into this inner resource. Leonardo da Vinci used a wide range of strategies to access the creative potential of his unconscious mind, including sitting for long periods staring blankly at a wall. He claimed this produced an inspirational dreamlike state in which creativity would effortlessly flow. Mozart too claimed to know an altered state where time and conscious effort ceased to exist, comparing his most inspirational moments to a 'pleasing and lively dream in which any conscious awareness became secondary'.

But this ability to access unconscious creativity and wisdom isn't restricted to the geniuses of the world; it's available to anyone. Most of us experience it without realizing.

Consider a man who needs to wake up at an unusual time, say 3:00 am. He sets his alarm clock to the appointed hour yet wakes up just before the alarm rings: the display reads 2:59 am. What made him wake up seconds before the appointed time? It certainly wasn't anything he was consciously doing, because he was asleep – by definition, unconscious.

Let's review what happened here. In the moment the alarm was set, a second internal alarm was also unconsciously set. A good night's sleep then followed until something happened in the unconscious mind which woke the sleeper just seconds before the alarm rang. Now here's the truly magical part: it achieved all this in relation to a clock that it can't see!

To fully appreciate how impressive this feat is, let's consider what might happen if we tackled the same problem from a conscious perspective. If we were asked to sit quietly in a room and consciously calculate when six hours had passed, how would we fare? Could we guess to within a minute? We'd do well to get within 20 minutes of the appointed time. However, the difference in these two examples lies in the fact that in the latter case we would consciously be trying hard to solve the problem and in the former we'd be trusting our unconscious mind to handle the details, which it does effortlessly.

There can be no doubt that humans have some kind of unseen and unconscious ability to self-heal. Evidence abounds of people who have somehow managed to heal themselves despite a bleak prognosis from doctors, through a process which medical experts are unable to explain. During the years we have spent running the Life Balance course, we have met many people who tell similar stories about how they'd been advised by specialists that they'd never walk again, yet there they were standing before us, providing clear evidence that the functioning of the physical body can be mysteriously and powerfully influenced by something that is taking place in the unconscious mind.

Such cases are fascinating and we always tried to learn more about each individual story. We were unable to discover how these people were able to self-heal so impressively, often in contradiction of overwhelming medical opinion, but we noticed they had one or two things in common with each other, not least of which was a steadfast, seemingly unrealistic refusal to accept the prognosis they'd been given. Whatever it is that generates self-healing, it seems to happen unconsciously, and by under-standing more about this non-rational inner resource we may therefore gain the wisdom to transform any area of our life.

There is a vitality, a life force, an energy that is translated through you into action and because there is only one of you in all time this expression is unique. If you block it, it will never exist through any other medium and will be lost forever. Martha Graham

II

Intuition will tell the thinking mind where to look next.
Dr Jonas Salk, discoverer of the polio vaccine

In 1989 an innovative book appeared called *Mindfulness*. The author, Ellen Langer, was the first woman tenured at Harvard University, and has an award for 'distinguished contributions to psychology in the public interest'. In the late 1970s she and C. Alexander began an experiment to measure the effects on physical ageing of a person's non-conscious acceptance of their deterioration in health.

An isolated venue in New England was refurbished to look exactly as it would in 1959. The radio and television played music and shows from that era, so that anyone living in the house would feel they were right back in that year. Langer and her colleagues gathered together a group of men in their seventies and eighties who had demonstrated health problems associated with ageing, such as loss of physical strength and joint flexibility, deterioration in vision and hearing, failing mental dexterity, and memory loss. These men were then divided into two groups; the first spent one week living together in the house watching programs and listening to music from 1959 – even the newspapers were authentic, carrying news items from that year. A second group, the 'control group', later spent a week in the house but in slightly different conditions: while they were encouraged to relax and enjoy living in '1959', they were constantly reminded that this was just a mock set of the period and in reality they were still living in the 1970s.

The results were extremely interesting. Both groups showed measurable improvements, both physically and mentally, but the first group, who were allowed to become totally immersed in and seduced by the experience, demonstrated greater improvement in every category. Their gait noticeably altered and in many cases finger length increased, indicating a decline in arthritic restriction. In IQ tests conducted when entering and leaving the program, 63% of participants in the first group had improved their test scores compared to 44% from the second control group. Perhaps the most noticeable change was in their physical appearance: when outside observers were shown photographs of the men leaving the program, they all agreed that each man looked younger than he had when he arrived.

This provides an excellent example of how effortlessly our unconscious mind creates change, both physically and mentally. It's unlikely that these men were consciously trying to feel younger; in fact they were probably doing nothing else than relaxing and enjoying the experience. Any change that took place happened because of something they were doing unconsciously. The unconscious mind controls our body and quickly initiates physical and mental change if it believes the information it receives – as evidenced by the powerful 'placebo effect'. Therefore, perhaps these results aren't too surprising. These men all became 'younger' and healthier, both physically and mentally, when their unconscious mind believed they were living in 1959.

The mind is a tool, a machine moved by spiritual fire.
Dostoevsky

We are indeed an enigmatic species defined by a mind that hasn't yet learned how to fully access the limit of its own vast potential, assuming a limit exists. The natural intuition we call 'sixth sense' provides another example of how a part of our being tries to guide and care for us. It seems we can effortlessly know when something is wrong even when the conscious focus of our attention is directed elsewhere, yet when we try to analyze how this happens we cannot explain it.

In his 2005 book *Blink*, Malcolm Gladwell introduced the term 'thin slicing' to describe humans' intuitive ability to read complex situations despite having very limited knowledge of them. Gladwell tells of a New York fireman who ordered his men out of a burning building, just moments before it exploded, because he sensed something was not quite right – the fire seemed to be *too hot*. The team was fighting a blaze in the kitchen of the house, unaware that a second more powerful fire was raging in the basement beneath their feet. Somehow this officer sensed something was wrong and, by acting on intuition, saved his own life and the lives of his crew. The building exploded just moments after they had left it.. Later, when asked why he gave the order to leave, or how he knew something was wrong, the officer couldn't say for sure; he said he just somehow seemed to know it.

Few would deny that such intuitive awareness exists and many have experienced it personally. This is no *conscious* effort for self-preservation; it is an entirely unconscious insight that shows up effortlessly, a deep-seated sense that all is not well. While many of us simply ignore it, the wisest among us are learning to recognize this inner wisdom for what it is and act accordingly, sometimes with life-changing consequences.

An integral being knows without going, sees without looking, and accomplishes without doing.
Lao Tzu

We all have this natural ability. We already know how to increase our self-esteem to create greater happiness and the life we really want, but we've simply lost touch with it. At our disposal is this most impressive and unconsidered resource, but it seems to have one critical flaw: it cannot tell the difference between what is real and what is vividly imagined. If it could make that distinction, we'd be unable to have a nightmare.

It's possible to wake up in the middle of a bad dream pouring with sweat, with a pounding heart and feelings of extreme stress. These physical fight/flight responses are not imagined; they're very real and affect us powerfully, because our conscious mind is switched off. The nightmare appears to be so real to our unconscious mind that it responds by initiating the intense and stressful reaction. If you saw the same images while awake – for example, if you could capture the visual images of the nightmare and watch them as a video – your physical and emotional response would be entirely different.

The part of our brain that controls our physical and emotional responses is very easily duped if the quality of a visualization is good enough, which is why my daughter and I kept trying to influence the direction of a car on a computer screen by turning our arms to steer. Clearly, the images we hold in our mind have great power to influence us, creating negative and positive emotions alike. We can look at this fact two different ways: first, it reminds us we can scare the heck out of ourselves with our imagination; second, we recognize that the same process must work both ways, therefore we can use it to produce positive outcomes if we know how to create the relevant imagery. We can't choose to opt out of the process, but we can choose to understand and reprogram it to create the emotions that best support our goals.

The intellect has little to do on the road to discovery. There comes a leap in consciousness, call it intuition or what you will, and the solution comes to you, and you don't know how or why.
Albert Einstein

Most of us rarely think about the way we condition our unconscious mind, freely allowing negative influences to filter in, then reacting with total surprise when they re-emerge to find expression in our emotional state. Yet by increasing our awareness of the programming process, we can introduce changes that effortlessly yield positive emotional results. We have far more autonomy in this subliminal area of our mind than we realize. After all, we weren't born with our unconscious programs set in place and they didn't arrive in the mail, therefore at some time in the past we set them up, albeit unintentionally. If it is possible to establish an unconscious program that initiates and sustains emotions of low self-esteem, it must also be possible to switch it off or remove it altogether. But to do this, we must first understand how it operates and what allows it to start up.

Feelings of low self-esteem or anxiety don't just show up; they need a trigger of some kind in order to begin. In many cases the trigger is something which occurs outside of our conscious awareness. We fail to notice the background music that initiates an unconscious association to a specific person or memory; perhaps we miss the subtle associations of freshly cut grass to events that took place long ago in a summer holiday of our youth. We may feel emotionally flat now for no apparent reason and search our *current* experiences in an effort to make sense of the situation while remaining completely unaware of the unconscious triggers that may have started the process an hour or more earlier.

Most people with anxiety issues cannot explain how they start up these programs because most of what they are doing takes place beyond their conscious awareness and without any conscious effort – since certainly no one would do it intentionally. Think about this for a moment; if we run those anxiety programs without any conscious effort, then surely we can run an opposite unconscious program just as effectively and effortlessly.

Why should we think our unconscious mind can only initiate unpleasant emotions? Can we believe that positive thinkers need to continuously work at staying positive, while their negative-thinking counterparts achieve the opposite results with ease and efficiency? It's more reasonable to assume we're dealing with a two-way process and that we can reprogram our unconscious mind to flow effortlessly in any direction.

People either don't understand this or are unwilling to believe it could be that simple. We are conditioned to believe anything worthwhile must be difficult to achieve, requiring a complicated strategy or hard conscious effort. Many of us try to overcome the debilitating effect of low self-esteem by conscious resistance. But while engaging our conscious mind to resist a specific negative emotion at one level, without realizing it we're effortlessly creating it and sustaining it at another. It is an unequal contest in which the winner is unlikely to be that of hard conscious effort, and this serves only to increase any sense of helplessness we had to begin with. This approach clearly won't be much use to someone who feels anxious; in fact few things are as frustratingly unproductive as this self-induced inner civil war. It seems the harder we try to resist negative emotions, the stronger they become. Anyone who has experienced the paralyzing effects of a panic attack will confirm that consciously trying hard to resist is not an effective strategy at all. It's been said that 'what we resist will persist'.

This doesn't mean we should give in to unwanted emotions such as panic; rather we should be mindful that hard conscious efforts to resist it may make us feel tense, and tension helps sustain it. This further fuels our anxieties, thus creating a negative self-perpetuating cycle of cause and effect. The way to break this negative cycle is by developing a sense of mindfulness and greater self-awareness. We are rarely powerless to resist our negative emotions. We'll be learning some coping strategies in later chapters that are effective in the short term, but our greatest power lies not in learning how to *cope* with these problems but in learning how to *solve* them.

Problem management is no more than the term suggests – a way of managing a problem; it's acceptable in the case of problems that can't be solved but anxiety issues almost always can be. A much more effective long-term solution lies in learning to re-program our unconscious mind to stop it creating these anxieties in the first place.

Trying to remedy a problem in one place while continuing to empower it in another is like collecting water from a leaky roof in a bucket. A long-term and sustainable solution can't be reached by continuously emptying the bucket. We could invest all our time and effort in learning to change the buckets faster and more efficiently, but we'd never be truly free of our core problem. The only truly effective way to create a long-term solution is by fixing the hole in the roof.

> There is a road from the eye to the heart that does not go through the intellect.
> G. K. Chesterton

The unconscious programs we run will override any conscious effort we make to resist. Someone with low confidence may try to fake confidence, hoping it might help in the short term, but it wouldn't be of much long-term benefit since their pre-set unconscious sense of self would continuously override any conscious efforts to bluff their way through permanently.

Throughout our lives we've been programming our unconscious to hold a certain sense of self-image, though most of us are unaware this conditioning has occurred. The unconscious identity we have created is now firmly in place. (It's certainly not *permanent*, though it remains so for many people because it doesn't receive much conscious attention.) This unconscious sense of self is extremely important because, like a compass, it guides us through life, continually influencing the direction we take.

Imagine we have a boat with an automatic pilot system; we want to go north, so we set the autopilot accordingly. Our boat will always travel north because it's been pre-programmed to do so. One day we decide we don't like going north – it's cold and cloudy and we feel we need some sunshine in our lives. We want our boat to sail south but we don't make any changes to the autopilot; instead we consciously take hold of the rudder and use it to steer a southerly course. In one sense we've achieved our goal: we're now heading south and will continue to do so as long as we remain where we are and keep hold of that rudder.

The flaw in this strategy is obvious: we can't stay there holding that rudder indefinitely – we have to eat, we have to sleep, we have to get up and move around – and the moment we let go of the rudder the boat is going to go north again because it has a pre-set program directing it to do so. In the same way, we have pre-set our own unconscious programs. Our 'direction' is influenced by our 'autopilot' until we consciously introduce a change, but conscious changes require effort to maintain and a lot of focused attention; whereas unconscious programs, once in place, allow us to forget the task in hand and place our conscious attention elsewhere.

Once established, our unconscious programs will run effortlessly and remain in place until something happens to override or interrupt them. This is why most people find change so difficult to create and sustain. Whether they try to stop smoking, lose weight, or increase self-esteem, the same principle applies: their efforts to change will be much harder if they use a strategy which requires them to consciously resist an unconscious program they're already running. Their focus is on the unwanted problem, and our unconscious mind always tries to explore and enhance what we consistently think about. In fact we can do much to help ourselves by directing our thoughts towards solutions rather than problems and we'll explore this notion in greater detail later.

All unconscious programs, whether positive or negative, must by definition operate effortlessly. Imagine how you would improve your self-esteem if you realized the process of change could be created as easily as you currently create low self-esteem. How much easier it would be to stop smoking or lose weight if the unconscious program that made it difficult was reversed! Positive, supportive emotions would then flow as easily as the negative ones currently do.

A mind once stretched by a great or new understanding will never fully return to its original dimensions.
William James

You may say: 'If it were that simple, surely we'd all be doing this already!' Yet it is that simple, and people are doing it already – they just don't realize they are. Some people find change easier to achieve than others. We may even know this type personally; they seem to be able to set a goal and stick to it, and also make it look infuriatingly simple. While others try to create change through hard conscious effort and willpower, these individuals sail successfully through the experience, claiming 'it was no big deal'.

How is this possible?

We all share the same neurological system, so these people obviously don't have some kind of an edge in that department. Something else must be going on inside their mind that is making all the difference. If we asked them what it was, they'd say they didn't know – maybe change just comes easily to them. But such people are not naturally gifted in a way the rest of us aren't. The difference lies in how they use their minds, albeit unconsciously.

Every emotion is created effortlessly. Our problems arise

when we become desperate either to resist a bad feeling or attain a good feeling. Happiness and love seem to become strangely elusive if we're desperate to find them, yet we are continuously surrounded by them and can access them any time we choose – as we will ultimately discover.

Unconscious self-esteem is created by rewriting the programs of our unconscious mind to automatically produce an empowering sense of self. If we set up an unconscious program to produce low self-esteem and allow it to remain in place, no amount of self-help techniques will ever free us from our trance of unworthiness. Milton Erickson captured the spirit of this struggle between our conscious and unconscious mind using the metaphor of horse and rider: the unconscious mind is the horse, and the conscious mind is the rider. Anyone who has ever seen a horse galloping off with a helpless rider clinging tightly to its neck may appreciate the similarity of consciously trying to resist an unpleasant emotion as it arises from the unconscious. Usually, the rider goes wherever the horse wants to go.

We all want to be happy. We could wear ourselves out trying hard to live a happy life, and yet all the while something within seems to override every effort we make to change direction. Unfortunately this sense of self-impediment will continue until the communication between 'horse' and 'rider' changes.

Creative thinking involves breaking out of established patterns in order to look at things in different ways.
Edward de Bono, author of *Lateral Thinking*

Consciously trying hard might be an effective strategy in pursuit of physical goals but it will be of little help in creating emotional or psychological change. In the following pages you will learn many different ways to unconsciously create and sustain change and access the creativity that empowers greater happiness. When taken to heart, this will transform more than your sense of self-esteem; it will also positively impact any area of your life that lacks balance and wholeness.

The path to greater happiness lies in wholeness and balance. These are the two most natural aspects of our being and we quickly begin to suffer when we ignore or move away from them. If we look closely, we see that people are basically good and the human spirit is sourced in love and peace, which means that we already have access to unconscious self-esteem and everything else we need – if only we can remember how to strengthen the natural connections with our true sense of self.

We can choose to ignore who we really are for the duration of our lives but our ignorance cannot separate us from our true self, just as choosing to ignore the presence of the moon wouldn't mean it ceased to exist. Who we really are remains constant at our center, whether we choose to acknowledge it or not.

Our goal is unconscious confidence and higher self-esteem, and the source of what we seek already exists inside us. This may be hard to believe right now, but in fact it cannot possibly be otherwise. Confidence and self-esteem, like all emotions, are created within, therefore the potential for any emotional change must also be within us. Just cultivating your awareness of this simple truth will liberate and change you, since it provides a subtle reminder to your unconscious mind that increased self-confidence and self-esteem are created from the inside out, requiring no consent other than your own.

The spirit is the true self.
Cicero (106–43 BC)

It has been said that the unconscious mind is the last great undis-covered region on this planet. Hopefully you have already made one discovery in realizing that within each of us lies an unlimited potential to create greater self-esteem and happiness.

We set out now as explorers to learn more about unconscious

confidence. Who knows? Somewhere along the path you may even discover your true self.

Quick Start: Resources

Questions

Take a look at the following eight questions:

1. What do I most want to change about myself?
2. When do I want to make this change?
3. How would I rather see myself?
4. What would my life be like if I were like that?
5. What would I be able to do that I don't do now?
6. What else?
7. Will I have to give up or lose anything when I make this change?
8. How much do I want this change now?

Consider each question in turn and see what shows up. Don't worry about trying to find a logical answer – just be aware of what springs to mind. You may find it helpful to write down your answers so that you can review what you wrote at various times between now and the end of the book.

2

Beliefs

Take the first step in faith. You don't need to see the whole staircase, just take the first step.
Dr Martin Luther King Jr

Some years ago I came across a survey which had invited people aged 65 or over to consider if, in their opinion, their life had been a success. Since the term 'success' means different things to different people, each person was told to base their answers entirely on their definition of the word. The results surprised me: 85% of those surveyed said they would not regard their life as a success.

Personally I expected the figures to be the reverse; after all, these people had reached at least 65 years of age – a feat in itself. Furthermore, anyone of that age at the time of the survey had made it through World War II in one piece. Why then would 85% of these people think their life hadn't been a success?

We can't ask them, but we do know that the way we think about ourselves influences what we believe is true, and what we believe is true influences how we think about ourselves. This cycle of cause and effect leaves its emotional legacy. If we have low self-esteem we will unconsciously initiate beliefs which support our low self-image. Those beliefs then further diminish our sense of self, thus perpetuating the cycle from within. Yet few people realize the unconscious influence that lies in what they believe to be true.

Our journey begins with our willingness to suspend what we have been led to believe is true about who we are and what we can achieve. For some, this may prove to be easier said than done, because beliefs are highly influential factors in our lives, providing the framework in which we make sense of our world. Suggesting that we should suspend our key beliefs for a while is like asking a jockey to release his hold on the reins of a horse at full gallop, but if we hope to create and keep the changes we seek, we must begin by relaxing these reins just a little.

Beliefs are essential ingredients in the recipe for change. They are true for the believer, empowering or disempowering. The 85% of people who believed life had been unsuccessful were almost certainly experiencing a different quality of happiness than the 15% who believed their life had been a success. Clearly it's much easier to feel happy if you believe you're living a full and successful life than if you believe it's been a huge disappointment. We can assume that the participants in the survey were unconsciously creating a lifestyle to match what they believed.

We tend to look at things with a negative or positive slant, habitually inclining towards one more than the other. Beliefs are actually neither right nor wrong – they simply move us in an emotional direction. They are like trains: they take us somewhere. If we don't like our emotional destination we can change it by altering what we believe is true.

Low self-esteem is the legacy of a story we've been telling ourselves over and over, but stories are easily internalized, and when they're repeated often enough the listener may start to believe they are true. The story of who we *believe* we are began long ago when we were children and is primarily based on early interactions with other people: parents, siblings, teachers – anyone we had any meaningful contact with. They all helped to write this story of identity that we've been unconsciously topping up ever since. The seeds of low self-esteem are easily planted and soon cultivated by a mind that learns to ignore the most important and nourishing information about itself. The debilitating habits of self-deprecation are established when we listen to the inner voice repeatedly telling us how unworthy and inadequate we are, and listing all that is wrong with our life. Many of us have been listening to this internal commentary for too long now; perhaps it's time for us to rewrite the script.

You can transcend all negativity when you realize that the only power it has over you is your belief in it. As you experience this truth about yourself you are instantly set free.
Eileen Caddy

The unique and subjective way we experience ourselves and our world plays a huge role in creating high self-esteem and a contented state of mind. High self-esteem also provides a key to create and maintain good physical health, and research has consistently shown a healthy sense of self to be an essential factor in healing and recovery following emotional trauma or depression. Many of the emotional maladies that commonly affect people in our society can be directly or indirectly connected to low self-esteem and a belief that we are not okay. During an anxiety attack, for example, the connection with negative beliefs becomes glaringly apparent.

A typical panic attack has a particularly powerful secret weapon: total surprise. It usually shows up without any warning and seemingly without reason. Its appearance is both debilitating and terrifying to the sufferer, but what is the underlying cause of this unpleasant experience? The principle ingredient in a panic attack is an underlying belief that we are in some way unsafe, and as this belief quickly escalates, a sense of anxiety gathers momentum. Recent studies have demonstrated that a healthy and strong sense of self significantly reduces the likelihood of future attacks by removing the unconsciously held sense that we are vulnerable or unsafe.

This type of 'I'm not okay' thinking is unconsciously developed over a period of time as a by-product of low self-esteem. By cultivating the belief that we are inadequate or lacking in value we create the perfect conditions in which future anxieties can unconsciously develop and thrive. So in truth panic attacks *don't* appear without good reason – they're initiated by the negative beliefs we have accumulated in our unconscious mind. Fortunately, there is a great deal we can change at that deeper level in order to help prevent such experiences from ever resurfacing. When we learn to cultivate a nurturing sense of self, accepting and loving ourselves, we remove the potential to develop these fear-based beliefs in the first place.

The essential driving force behind conditions such as OCD (obsessive compulsive disorder) is a belief that something negative will happen to us unless we complete specific behavioral tasks in a particular way. This trance of fear might require us to switch lights on and off a number of times on leaving a room, or to undertake other specific rituals to avoid any negative consequences to ourselves or those we love. By surrendering to these demands we become victims of a fear-based belief, but yet again if we look beneath the surface of the problem we find low self-esteem driving these behaviors.

Of course, not all unpleasant emotions are the result of fear; some show up as warnings. We should try to recognize the underlying intention, since they may be our unconscious mind's way of protecting us from harm, especially if we engage in a lifestyle that may ultimately be bad for us. Perhaps a key aspect of our system is out of balance or lacking harmony with the whole, and that negative emotion is drawing our attention to something that needs to change within our lifestyle.

Perceive all conflict as patterns of energy seeking harmonious balance as elements in a whole.
Dyhani Ywahoo, Etowah Cherokee

Since beliefs so powerfully affect our self-image, our opening gambit must be to renegotiate our contract with reality and review the beliefs we have learned to meekly accept as facts. In this chapter we'll explore where our beliefs come from and what might happen if we decide to challenge them, and we begin by challenging a belief that is more damaging to our unconscious sense of self than any other: the notion that happiness and self-worth are created externally.

If we try to create emotional change from the outside, we may be seduced into a trance of external reference in which we become convinced that we can make ourselves happier through material acquisition or the good opinion of others. It's easy to get sucked into this illusion because we live in a world where we are continuously encouraged to believe this very thing! You need only turn on your TV to see an advert suggesting the latest sofa will create greater happiness in your life. On the surface it might seem true: that sofa does look very nice and the person sitting on it looks even nicer. But at a deeper level of awareness we know this belief is flawed and unable to provide long-term change; it might make us a little happier right now in the short term, but if we go out shopping to feel better today, we'll need another dose of that retail therapy tomorrow just to top up the feeling.

Believing that long-term happiness can be created by external objects is a crazy idea that disempowers the creativity of our unconscious mind. We are the only ones who can create greater contentment in our lives – it's always an 'inside job'. The main flaw in seeking happiness externally is that it often results in an underlying sense of dissatisfaction that leads to further unhappiness. If we search for self-fulfillment in the good opinion of others, we may wear ourselves out trying to find it and become anxious that we're not creating enough external praise. Equally, if we believe we are not keeping up in the race for material gain, this may create a further drop in our unconscious self-image.

I was always looking outside myself for strength and confidence but it comes from within, and it was there all the time.
Anna Freud (1895–1982)

Sadly, too many of us do believe happiness is created externally so we look for it there, which is like looking in the wrong place for something you've lost. You wouldn't dream of looking in the fridge for the TV remote because you don't believe it's in there. Similarly if we believe we don't have the inner resources to create self-esteem and happiness we're unlikely to look inside ourselves to find them. What we believe always influences where we look for solutions to problems, therefore it is in our beliefs that the path to greater happiness and self-empowerment must begin.

As our insights ripen and our capacity for self-empowerment becomes evident, we unconsciously begin to access our inner resources for change. It can be a liberating and surprising experience to discover how different you can feel simply by challenging one or two of your limiting beliefs or by making a small change in the way you see yourself. Solutions can somehow become obvious, as if they have been there all the time just waiting to be noticed. It is a strange irony that every form of talking therapy requires the therapist to find solutions by asking questions of the one real expert in the room. The solutions exist already in the unconscious mind of the patient; the therapist simply empowers them to come to the surface. The solutions within us will flow more readily into our awareness if we cultivate the kind and nurturing energy of high self-esteem.

We possess the amazing capacity to influence ourselves in a multitude of ways. At a deeper level we know intuitively what we need, how much of it we need, and when we need it. No one else can know you as intimately as you know yourself; no one can ever tune into your inner wisdom as effectively as you can. The fact is, you're the only person in this world who could ever get a PhD in the subject of your life.

Realization of this simple truth is the beginning of change.

Story

An ancient Eastern myth tells how the gods held the secret of the universe but wanted to hide it in a place where man would never find it. One god suggested hiding it in the deepest ocean, but it was agreed that it was only a matter of time before man became smart enough to build a craft that would take him to the bottom of any ocean.

Another god suggested hiding the secret out in space on the surface of a far-flung planet, but again the general opinion was that man would eventually develop a spaceship to take him to the edges of the universe.

Finally the perfect, safest place was found. The gods agreed they would hang it round the neck of every human being because people would never think of looking for the secret of life in such an obvious place.

* * *

You already know how to create greater happiness in your life, and your sense of intuitive awareness will ripen as we learn more about this natural process of self-actualization. As soon as we start to see ourselves from a different perspective and recognize our beliefs for what they really are, we empower a liberating, life-changing experience. It's important to remember that what we believe about ourselves is neither wrong nor right. Beliefs either help us or they don't; they keep us small and fearful or they empower us to live our lives at the outer edges of our potential, and it's up to you to decide which beliefs belong in which category.

Almost everyone has at least one belief that holds them back. Young children in school may believe they can't do mathematics or science yet in most cases it isn't a lack of ability that keeps them stuck; it's what they believe is true about their ability. Letting go of our most limiting beliefs can sometimes be difficult because they have usually been there with us from such an early age. Many intelligent adults genuinely believe they are poor learners or that they can't spell or do basic arithmetic. They may have established these beliefs a long time ago but the negative effect continues to undermine their sense of self-esteem. How and where did we learn this trance of self-limitation? Were we born with these beliefs or did we at some point in our childhood mindlessly allow the seeds of someone else's negative communication to take root and flourish in the fertile soil of our unconscious mind?

Shrug off the restraints that you have allowed others to place upon you.
You are limitless; there is nothing you cannot achieve.
There is no sadness in life that cannot be reversed.
Clearwater

Since beliefs tend to become self-fulfilling prophecies, we must be careful what we believe is true, not only about ourselves but also about others. Let me share with you an example of how powerfully our beliefs can distort our thinking.

A substitute professor at Harvard was introduced to his class with a written biographical statement providing some background information about him. However, one half of the students were given a handout which described the lecturer as 'rather cold', while the other half's handout described him as 'very warm'. The whole class received exactly the same lecture, yet in their reviews of the professor the half who had received the 'very warm' statement all rated him as 'good natured, very considerate of others, informal, sociable, popular, humorous, and humane', in stark contrast to the other half, who rated him 'self centered, formal, unsociable, unpopular, irritable, humorless,

32

and ruthless' (H. H. Kelley, 'The Warm/Cold Variable in First Impressions of Persons', *Journal of Personality*, 1950, 18, 431–439).

The students had no idea how powerfully their beliefs had influenced their opinions about the professor and shaped their experience. This was no case of deliberate discrimination; their perception of the man was influenced by beliefs they held *unconsciously*, and so they were completely unaware of their effect. The beliefs that you and I hold unconsciously are also influencing every decision we make, not just about other people but most importantly about who we think we are and what we think we can do. Our biggest problem is that we are doing all this unconsciously yet the limiting effects show up in real life.

It is helpful to remember that what we believe about ourselves may not be true. The problem occurs when we regard a limiting belief as a fact rather than an idea with no supporting proof. A fact is something we *know* is true whereas a belief is an idea we have learned to accept as true without bothering to check it out. The dictionary definition of the word 'belief' generally reads as follows: 'a principle accepted as true, especially without proof'. Therefore by definition we cannot regard the negative things we believe about ourselves as facts; they're no more than ideas we have accepted without any evidence.

If you believe you're a reasonably open-minded person, you might consider for a moment what it would be like to see a limiting belief from the flip side.

Exercise

Think of a belief you have about yourself that consistently limits you in some way. (Make sure you choose a belief, not a fact. A fact is something you *know for sure* is true.)

Hold that belief in your mind for a moment, and listen to your internal voice stating it.

What kind of emotional experience did that belief create for you?

Now, take that limiting belief, and 'flip it over'. In other words, allow yourself to believe for a few moments that the opposite belief is true. If my limiting belief was, 'I'm not a good learner', I'd change it to 'I'm an excellent learner'.

What did you experience as a result of this flip-over? Whatever you felt, just notice it and be aware that *you* are the one who created it. We can't alter the fact that our beliefs influence our unconscious mind but we can choose what we believe, and that is a powerful understanding to have in the journey of change.

If you believe you can or you believe you can't, in either case you're probably right.
Henry Ford

What we believe also determines how we think about our goals. The moment we choose to believe we can achieve something, it becomes easier to see ourselves in the outcome. If we then hold that picture in our imagination, we activate a part of our brain that helps us move towards our goal. This is why visualization exercises are highly regarded in pursuit of sporting excellence.

Throughout history people from a wide variety of backgrounds have been able to dramatically alter the course of their lives simply by challenging what they'd been led to believe was true about themselves and their abilities. Introducing this simple shift in awareness generates a powerful sense of unstoppable energy for change. Can it be coincidental that some people die shortly after they retire, or could it be due to an unconscious shift in the way they perceive themselves, their purpose in life, and their contribution to society? A belief that we are past our 'sell-by date' must strongly influence us at an unconscious level and may affect our physical health and general state of mind. We must cultivate and sustain a healthy sense of self and purpose if we hope to live a long, healthy life and feel content and fulfilled.

Men are disturbed not by things that happen, but by their beliefs about the things that happen.

Epictetus

People sometimes find it easier to alter their beliefs if something happens to inspire them or if they get feedback from their world suggesting their opinions were wrong. However, we could grow old and grey waiting for one of these options to show up in our life. In truth it's never too late for us to change what we believe is true about ourselves or our ability.

Story

She was 58 years old and enjoyed a good life, but she hadn't achieved much outside the home. She had never learned to drive and had never been employed, not even part time.

One day her daughter asked her to look after the two grandchildren for a while and of course she was delighted to do so. Some time later, the little boy ran into the house, screaming that his sister was in trouble, and this 58-year-old grandmother rushed outside to find her precious granddaughter trapped under the wheels of a car. The children had been playing hide-and-seek under it when the brake came off and the vehicle rolled backward over the girl, pinning her to the ground.

This woman had two choices: she could stand there and watch her granddaughter die, or she could try to move the car – but it was locked, and anyway she didn't know how to drive. Faced with this critical choice, she did the only thing she could: she tried to lift the car. She managed to lift it just enough to enable her grandson to pull the girl from under the wheels, and then she dropped it.

Neighbors had witnessed this amazing event and it wasn't long before the news media appeared on the woman's doorstep. Yet for some reason she refused to give an interview; she wouldn't speak about it to anyone.

Two years later, an author who was collecting information for a book about unusual human achievements asked to interview her, but she refused. Eventually, he went to her home and begged her to explain why she was so reluctant to talk about what had happened.

She replied that she had never achieved much in her life. Then that day came and she had done something she believed was totally impossible. Once the dust began to settle, it struck her that if she could do something like that – something she believed was impossible – what else could she have achieved in her life, if only she had believed it was possible? This thought depressed her. She wished she had known this liberating information when she was 16, not at 60, when it was too late.

The author asked what she would have done differently if she had known this at 16. She replied that she'd always been passionate about geology; she had books on the subject, and wished she had done a degree in it when she was younger, but now of course she was too old, and it was too late.

He pointed out that there was a nearby college offering degree courses to students of all ages. She could enroll today for a five-year degree in geology.

'Have you been listening to me?' she asked. 'I'm 60 years old! If I start that course now, how old will I be in five years when I graduate?'

He thought for a moment and said, 'How old will you be in five years' time if you don't?'

She did enroll, and graduated five years later.

* * *

This is a true story, providing a reminder to us all that we are never too old to do something different, and challenging us to think about the powerful factors that altered the direction of this woman's life. It seems her life changed because she changed what she believed was true, about herself and her ability to create the life she really wanted.

Perhaps you are wondering about *your* beliefs and how they are currently serving you. Are they empowering you to create the life you want and the happiness you deserve? Or are they holding you back, keeping you smaller than you really are? It's up to you to choose what you believe about yourself and your world and you must choose wisely, because your choice influences your entire life.

As human beings our greatness lies not so much in our ability to remake the world ... as in our ability to remake ourselves.
Mahatma Gandhi

Our journey will end with an increased sense of balance, happiness and love, but it begins here in challenging our beliefs about what is possible in our life.

In moments of self-doubt, you may choose to revisit these kind and empowering words by Marianne Williamson, which remind us of the person we really are.

Our deepest fear is that we are powerful beyond measure.
It is our light, not our darkness that most frightens us.
You are a child of God, your playing small does not serve the
world.
There is nothing enlightening about shrinking,
So that other people won't feel insecure around you.
We are born to make manifest the glory that is within us.
It is not just in some of us, it is in everyone, and as we let our
light shine,
We unconsciously give other people permission to do the same.
As we are liberated from our own fear, our presence automat-
ically liberates others.
Marianne Williamson, *A Return to Love*

It may be foolish to believe anything is possible, yet it is equally foolish to remain in a belief system that impairs our ability to create the quality of life we really want. Many of us have set our sights far below our true ability, and since life tends to live up to our expectations we may do well to become a little more optimistic.

Take a moment now to reflect on the way you currently see yourself, who you believe you are, and what you believe might become possible for you in the future.

What limiting beliefs could you change right now?

What will your life be like when you do change what you believe?

'There's no use trying,' she said. 'One can't believe impossible things.'

'I dare say you haven't had much practice,' said the Queen. 'When I was your age I always did it for half an hour a day. Why, sometimes I've believed as many as six impossible things before breakfast.'

Lewis Carroll, *Through the Looking Glass*

Quick Start: Resources
Challenge limiting beliefs with questions
When the self-doubts emerge and/or your internal critic starts up, ask yourself any or all of the following three questions:

1. Do I know this [negative belief] for a fact or is it just something I believe?
2. What would I like to be true about myself in this situation?
3. What would I be able to do if I felt happy and confident in this situation?

3

Watching the Wheels

We don't understand the operations of our minds, hence we don't operate them very well.
Charles Tart

Day two at the Life Balance course. We were about ten minutes in when she decided to share her insights with the group: 'If I'm totally honest, I don't think I like myself very much.'

She wasn't the only one with such a negative self-image; at least four others were sagely nodding in silent appreciation. If we'd heard it once, we'd heard it a hundred times before in previous groups: someone would raise the point then several others would demonstrate a sense of relief that they weren't alone in their illusion of worthlessness.

They were a standard group: five or six people each doing their best to get their life back on track. What they all mainly wanted was an increase in self-confidence, and in most cases this was obvious from the moment they walked through the door. Somewhere along the way, life had been less than kind, giving their self-confidence a severe knock, but there was this other shared factor, which was far more relevant to their situation yet nowhere near as obvious: they didn't like themselves very much.

Interestingly, the people we met who wanted more self-confidence had usually spent a lot of time and effort trying to create it, without much success, yet in almost every case their self-confidence quickly and dramatically increased as soon as they improved their self-esteem. This was either pure coincidence or clear evidence that if you develop greater self-esteem, you generate a powerful shift in self-confidence. To understand what allows this improvement to happen, we need to look beneath the surface of conscious awareness to discover how we unconsciously create self-esteem.

Self-esteem is founded on an unconsciously held notion of who *we think we are*, but as we shall see, the way we construct this idea of self may be inaccurate and invalid. You are the only person who will ever know exactly what it's like to be you; other people can imagine what it *might* be like, but they'll never match your experience exactly because the reality you create is unique and available only to you. We each live in an exclusive perceptual experience we label 'reality'; of course we all live in the same world but we experience it differently. You already know this but it is very easy to forget, and start believing that everyone sees things much the same way as you do. This of course is impossible – our individual perception of the world is as unique as our fingerprints.

At each level of perception things change dramatically. When you take your dog out for a walk, the dog has a very different experience from you because it smells things you can't smell (thankfully). Of course you and your dog are both moving around the same geographical location at the same time, but you're each processing it differently. If you and your friend go to the theater, your friend might leave thinking it was the worst show he had ever seen, yet you might be so impressed you see it again three times. Was your friend watching a different show from you? No, but you reacted differently because you each gave it a different meaning by unconsciously interpreting the information in your own unique way and so created your own reality.

Our five senses provide the primary filters through which we experience our world, and how we unconsciously use them influences how we form and sustain our unconsciously held sense of self. If we want to improve our sense of self-esteem we must understand that the sensory filters we use to create it don't furnish us with an accurate experience of our reality; they merely provide our *subjective interpretation* of it. This uniquely subjective perspective is often referred to as a 'map' by practitioners of neuro-linguistic programming (NLP), signifying that our experience of the world is neither accurate or real : it is only real to the observer of it. A map can never *be* the territory it describes, in much the same way as a picture can never really *be* the person.

There's a famous story about a man who wanted Pablo Picasso to paint his wife's portrait. He showed the artist a small snapshot, saying 'That's my wife.' Picasso studied the picture for a moment and said, 'She's very small, isn't she? And extremely flat.' It seems in art, as in life, perception is everything. Years spent habitually perceiving ourselves in a one-dimensional way might lead us to wonder what the world really looks like or who we really are, and of course the simple answer to these questions depends entirely on *who* is doing the looking and *how* they unconsciously interpret what they see.

No one can make you feel inferior without your permission.
Eleanor Roosevelt

Since self-esteem is entirely filter-dependent we can begin to improve it by challenging the reliability and accuracy of our sensory filters. We already know that beliefs are not reliable indicators of who we are or what we can achieve; are our sensory filters any more dependable as witnesses to our reality?

Let's begin by exploring the evidence provided by our visual filters.

We take what we see for granted, largely accepting the evidence provided by our eyes as accurate reflections of who and where we are, yet the evidence is far from accurate and not always reliable. Our eyes suggest the sun rises in the east and travels across the sky, eventually setting in the west, but everyone knows this isn't true: the sun hasn't moved much in relation to us since we saw it yesterday. The same visual filters inform us that we are primarily surrounded by empty space, yet we know there are no empty spaces in our world; the apparently empty space contains the air that we breathe to stay alive. These and all other related illusions arise because we rely too heavily on the evidence of our eyes, disregarding whatever we don't see. Yet the most beautiful aspect of human beings is invisible to the naked eye, and if we go through life judging people only by their physical appearance we miss the energy of love that lies beneath. The forces of nature such as gravity and electricity remain invisible to human sight but, like the unseen energy of love, they impact every aspect of our existence.

Strictly speaking, we don't actually 'see' anything at all. When we 'see', we are actually viewing an image that we have constructed in our mind. Sadly, most of us tend to forget this and fall into the illusion that what we see exists exactly as we see it.

What occurs around you and within you reflects your own mind, and shows you the dream you are weaving.
Dhyani Ywahoo

Our eyes gather information, which then arrives in the 'cinema' of our brain. Here we construct an image, much like a hologram, though this image seems so realistic that unfortunately we forget it exists only in our mind. In reality, what we see is not 'out there'; it's an *image* of what's out there. It's based on reality but it isn't reality. We all share the same neurology and sensory filter system yet any two people in the same situation will usually see things slightly differently from each other.

We've all heard the sort of conversation that runs, 'Oh, doesn't that guy look just like Steve?' to which someone else replies, 'What? He doesn't look anything like Steve at all!'

Both parties are sure they either did or didn't see someone like Steve, and they're both absolutely right. Perhaps you remember being surprised back in your school days when you discovered your friend was dating a person you considered totally unattractive. It may seem clear to you now that your friend saw something you didn't, or vice versa. In a courtroom we may listen to several witnesses giving an account of a crime, and wonder if they are all describing the same event. Of course it's a good thing that our sensory filters work this way or we might find ourselves trying to live in the same house, do the same job, and marry the same person as everyone else, which would be slightly inconvenient – so *vive la différence*!

A menu cannot ever *be* the food it describes; we wouldn't think of eating it anymore than we'd try to have a meaningful conversation with a photograph. Yet we allow ourselves to regard what we see in the mirror as an accurate representation of ourselves rather than merely our subjective interpretation. If our interpretation becomes distorted it will establish the foundations for low self-esteem, since it encourages a belief that everyone else sees us in the same negative light that we see ourselves. Our sensory filters unconsciously influence the way we develop and sustain our sense of self-esteem, which suggests we can improve it by changing how we process the information passing through our sensory system. In fact, even small perceptual shifts can generate huge changes.

This idea is demonstrated by three simple facts:

1. Self-esteem is unconsciously created as a result of *how* we perceive ourselves.
2. Perception changes when we change *how* we perceive ourselves.
3. When we change *how* we perceive ourselves, our self-esteem must also change.

When you change the way you look at things, the things you look at change.
Dr Wayne Dyer

In every seed lies the promise of a thousand forests, yet only we can plant the first seeds of change. When we remain mindful of this, our insights begin to ripen and we perceive the seeds of opportunity in every event we experience. At first it may seem unrealistic to ask us to challenge the reliability of our eyes after years of being accustomed to seeing ourselves in one particular way, yet this is how we begin to awaken our unconscious potential. We're all capable of making this perceptual shift and it doesn't have to take long; in fact it can happen in less than a heartbeat.

The first step in this transformation lies in the awareness that we only see our world subjectively. We've become quite skilled in the art of visual deception, especially with regard to our physical appearance. Consider how a woman suffering from anorexia can visually deceive herself. We may try to persuade her she's thin, assuring her that the overweight image she sees in the mirror is just an illusion in her mind, but she won't believe it because like everyone, she has become good at creating her own unique picture of who she thinks she is. She has learned to trust entirely in the flawed illusion of her sensory-based filters. The greatest conscious effort on our part to invalidate that self-image in the mind of the anorexic will be useless, yet this negative illusion of self can be quickly and effectively altered if the sufferer under-stands how to introduce even the smallest changes in the way her mind unconsciously processes incoming information.

To see a world in a grain of sand,
And a heaven in a wild flower,
Hold infinity in the palm of your hand,
And eternity in an hour ...
We are led to believe a lie
When we see not thro' the eye,
Which was born in a night to perish in a night
When the soul slept in beams of light.
William Blake

This may at first seem difficult, since we use our eyes in a largely unconscious way, giving little or no conscious thought to the majority of what is visually available. We unconsciously filter what we see into a narrow stream of incoming information, allowing in anything that supports our beliefs while excluding anything that may challenge them. We do this without any conscious awareness and we are extremely consistent, especially about the person we believe we see in our mirror. We can only allow our self-esteem to be influenced by what we see there if we trust our visual filters to provide objective facts – but we can't trust them.

An effective way to challenge our visual evidence is to introduce as much flexibility as possible. This simply means we cultivate the habit of asking ourselves if we can see things from any other perspective. Not only does this simple shift challenge our old fixed ideas of how the world works; it also helps us to think differently and be more open-minded.

We need only look at something in a slightly different way to create a big difference in how we think about it. Sometimes just the smallest perceptual shift will shatter our self-imposed illusion of unworthiness and let us realize that our physical body is only a small part of who we really are.

Body is that portion of the soul that can be perceived by the five senses.
William Blake

The key to sustainable change lies in doing something different. This may seem like common sense, but when it comes to creating change, common sense isn't very common! Einstein said the definition of insanity is to expect a different outcome from the same behavior: if you always do what you've always done, you'll always get what you've always had.

Surely it can't be that easy to alter how we feel about

something, just by looking at it differently! Logic suggests we could look at ourselves in any number of ways but still remain the same person – which of course is quite true. What changes, however, is the information that arrives in our conscious awareness because of the subtle shift in our perception; this, after all, is what makes the difference in each person's subjective view of the world. When we change the way we look at things, the things we look at really do change, including our perception of self.

Take a moment to read the following sentence from start to finish:

FINISHED FILES ARE THE
RESULT OF YEARS OF SCIENTIFIC
STUDY COMBINED WITH THE
EXPERIENCE OF MANY YEARS.

Now read the sentence again, and this time count the number of times the letter F occurs in it.

Whatever your answer, how sure are you that you are right? Are you 50% certain? Or higher – 75%, 90%? Perhaps you are even 100% sure.

You may indeed be right, but before we find out, let me invite you to explore how quickly things change when you look at them *differently*.

If you read the sentence again in a different way, you may discover something you missed the first time. For example, you could read it in reverse: start at the end of the sentence and read each *word* backwards, counting the Fs as you read.

Did anything change when you read it backwards? How many Fs are there now?

As you may now realize, there are no fewer than six Fs in that sentence.

What changed here was not the object of your vision but the

information you generated as a result of *how* you used your vision. If you saw all six Fs the first time, that's fine. But if you missed a few, consider this: if we can miss the information contained in a simple four-line sentence, how much more information might we miss as we unconsciously compile the complex quantum soup we call our world, our life, or, perhaps most importantly, our image of ourselves?

You spend more time with yourself than with any other person, therefore it makes sense to develop the kind of relationship in which you feel love, value and respect for yourself. If that idea seems repulsive to you right now, consider how you might feel if you took the opposite approach. If you lived your life holding feelings of disrespect and hate for yourself, would that work out for you more effectively?

Wisdom tells me I am nothing,
Love tells me I am everything.
And between the two my life flows.
Nisargadatta Maharaj

No one is born with low self-esteem. It's an opinion learned over time, and in order to develop and keep it in place we must first of all cultivate an unconscious ability to tune out all communication which contradicts our negative self-image while simultaneously noticing everything that may support it. Then, once we have set our unconscious mind to filter information this way, it will continue to do so automatically. As long as nothing interferes with the program, it will resist all conscious efforts to see ourselves from any other perspective.

Now of course, no one would ever set this process up intentionally, but since low self-esteem is created internally and without any conscious effort, it surely follows that there is an unconscious program running which allows it to continue.

Cultivating a healthy sense of self-esteem redirects our

unconscious filters to process incoming data in a different way. We suddenly start noticing things about ourselves that we had learned to filter out. Long-forgotten skills and positive aspects of our life slowly re-emerge in our awareness; we begin to feel an energy of transformation in everything! The programs that run in our unconscious mind begin to work in the opposite direction, filtering for information that confirms and supports our new self-image, while ignoring anything that undermines it. Trying to develop a healthy self-image while a conflicting image keeps popping into our mind can be frustratingly difficult, but through this less direct approach we undermine our negative sense of self by altering the perspective we have become accustomed to seeing it from. This doesn't mean we must try to discover something to like about ourselves through our existing unconscious filters; it simply means we need do little more than relax and take a different viewpoint of our world.

Many people change their mind, often becoming wiser with age. It's unlikely that you hold exactly the same opinions that you held 10 or 20 years ago, and in each instance you probably altered your opinion as a result of new information – perhaps you learned something that empowered you to respond in a different way. Likewise, when you discover something new about yourself, a change in the way you see yourself not only becomes possible but in most cases unavoidable. Such discoveries are the product of flexible thinking and to access them we must practice seeing things, including ourselves, from as many different perspectives as possible.

If you are feeling reasonably flexible right now, try the following exercise.

Exercise

Think of an activity you are good at, something you enjoy doing, the kind of thing that makes time stand still, and you feel like you're 'in the zone'.

Imagine yourself doing that activity now; pause for a few seconds to imagine it clearly.

Notice how good you feel when you are doing this activity.

Now think of someone who loves you unconditionally; this can be anyone at all as long as they love and accept you completely, just the way you are.

Imagine this person is watching you from a little distance away as you do your activity, without you being aware of their presence.

Step back for a moment and observe the two people in this picture: one of them is you, fully engaged in what you are doing, unaware you're being watched through loving eyes; notice also the loving and kind expression on the face of the person watching you.

Now shift your perception into that other person's mind for a moment and see yourself as they see you, through their eyes. As you do this, notice what it's like to see yourself entirely through their perceptual filters. Fully experience what that is like.

What do they see? What pleasant thoughts are they thinking as they watch you?

Notice what kind of feelings they have. How do you feel as you see yourself through their eyes?

Shifting your point of perception provides valuable insights about who you are when seen through the filters of unconditional love. This simple exercise allows you to alter the way you see yourselfand step beyond the limitations of your unconscious filters.. If you return to this exercise later, notice how your sense of self is beginning to change, effortlessly. Have you discovered something about yourself? Consider what now seems possible as a result of your discovery.

In my solitude
I have seen things very clearly,
that were not true.
Antonio Machado, 1983

Flexibility of thought keeps us beyond the reach of self-destructive beliefs about our world and the role we play in it. In our darker moments of self-abuse, we remember that the person we are abusing is no more than an illusion of our subjective reality. In cultivating our awareness of this liberating truth we break free of the self-imposed trance of worthlessness in which low self-esteem flourishes, and create the potential for greater happiness, harmony and balance in our lives. Exploring how we use our senses to experience our world provides the essential first step in renegotiating what, for many, has become an unproductive and outdated contract with reality.

Quick Start: Resources

Questions

When you feel blocked or stuck, ask yourself the following six questions:

1. How many different ways could I see this situation?
2. What does it mean?
3. What else does it mean?
4. What can I do differently now?
5. When have I encountered similar problems in the past?
6. How did I get over those problems at that time?

4

The Power of Unconscious Attraction

Every journey has a secret destination of which the traveler is unaware.
Martin Buber

'You are what you eat,' my friend smiled knowingly at me as she arranged various packs of fruit in her shopping trolley. She's probably right. In fact there's a British television program with that title which encourages us to give serious thought to what we eat and the effect it might have on our body. Of course, we have to eat – it's not optional – and programs that teach us how to eat healthily may help us live longer, happier lives. But there's something else that could help us live longer, happier lives. Like food, it powerfully affects us, though there are no television programs about it.

What is it?

Thinking.

We spend the majority of our time thinking We all have to think, just as we all have to eat, but there's something very important about the process of thinking that we should be aware of because it affects our lives whether we realize it or not.

Put simply, *We attract what we think about.*

What we think about influences us at every level of our being: relationships, work and, most importantly, our unconsciously held sense of self. We only have to change the way we think about something and our relationship with it changes instantly. We may think someone is physically attractive until we learn something distasteful about them, at which point they seem to become physically unattractive. Yet they're still the same person

– they haven't altered in any way physically; we are simply thinking about them from a different perspective now. When we change the way we think about things, the things we think about change, which means we have the power to change our lives by changing the way we think. It is that simple and we can all do it; but we don't, because it requires us to understand a part of our mind we give little or no thought to.

The idea that we attract what we think about may seem hard to accept. Admittedly, thinking about winning the lottery is unlikely to produce that outcome; likewise if you spend your time thinking about being married to a Hollywood film star you'll probably end up disappointed and for good reasons. Although your mind can do some amazing things, it's unlikely to be able to influence a computer that selects winning lottery numbers, or the emotions of a person in Hollywood. Your mind has limited power to influence external events or other people's lives, but it can influence *your* life. It does so as a result of what you consistently show it.

Think about this from another angle. Think of someone you know who is very happy, a person who is not just good at making themselves happy but also creates happiness in others. If you looked closely, you'd see that their thoughts consistently mirror their life experiences. Conversely, someone who continually complains that life's a bitch and that other people seem to get all the luck generally attracts life outcomes that match their communication.

The idea that we attract what we think about is not new yet remains largely ignored despite several highly acclaimed books on the subject. In *The Secret*, Rhonda Byrne introduces us to a number of well-respected and accredited individuals who provide a wealth of supporting evidence for this concept.

In *The Intention Experiment: Use Your Thoughts to Change the World*, Lynne McTaggart demonstrates how thoughts create measurable outcomes on a physical plane sometimes hundreds of miles away from the geographical location of the thinker. In his 1902 book *As a Man Thinketh*, James Allen provided clear evidence that we are the sum of our thoughts and can powerfully alter our lives by changing our thinking. Allen's book is regarded today as one of the self-help classics of the 20th century.

In *The Power of Your Subconscious Mind* (1963), Dr Joseph Murphy explains how we can change our lives by changing the landscape of our mind: 'Whatever is impressed into your subconscious mind is expressed on the screen of space. This idea was proclaimed by Moses, Isaiah, Jesus, Buddha, Zoroaster, and all the illuminated seers of the ages.' In her 1978 book *Creative Visualization*, Shakti Gawain shows how life tends to reflect the thoughts we have about it, whether positive or negative.

The recurring message of these books is that thoughts are a form of energy that finds physical or emotional expression in our lives. Many of the world's greatest thinkers have understood this and used it to positive effect, including Shakespeare, Sir Isaac Newton, Ralph Waldo Emerson, Victor Hugo, Beethoven, Leonardo da Vinci, Plato and Socrates. We're unlikely to find this idea on a school curriculum but our ability to understand it will make the difference between having the life we want and the life we don't want.

All that we are is a result of what we have thought.
Buddha (563–483 BC)

Our planet is home to a rich diversity of cultures, yet the idea that we attract what we think about shows up all over the world and is found in the texts of humankind's most ancient teachings. The Rig Veda, a Sanskrit text compiled around 1500 BC, conveys the message that we can change our lives by changing our thoughts. While these words are thousands of years old, they continue to provide a source for creating greater happiness and health today. Ayurvedic spa treatments, now commonplace in our culture, are founded on the ancient wisdom of these Vedic texts; the Sanskrit word ayurveda means 'wisdom of life'.

We may find the idea of unconscious attraction difficult to accept because our analytical mind demands logical proof, yet our world abounds with other inexplicable mysteries. How can identical twins separated by thousands of miles sense when their sibling is in danger? How do Pacific salmon spend years traversing the oceans and then find their way back to the place in the river where they were born years before? How can a bird bury food over a wide area of land then return months later to find it under a landscape transformed by thick snow? When we consider these expressions of unconscious intelligence, we begin to realize there's so much about ourselves and our world that we don't fully understand. Does it then seem so hard to believe that our unconscious mind attracts what we consistently think about? We live in a universe of endless possibilities, and our thoughts are the currency we use to purchase both our emotional outcomes and our sense of self.

Your imagination is the preview to life's coming attractions.
Albert Einstein

Consider these questions: If you were convinced beyond any doubt that you attract whatever you think about, what would you think about? More importantly, what do you think about now that you would immediately stop thinking about?

'As you think, so shall you be' is a saying that suggests our thoughts will find physical or emotional expression in our life. Since we have to think *something*, perhaps we should think about what we want rather than what we don't want. Consider what kind of internal energy we might be creating with thoughts of resentment or anger. Sometimes we feel justified in our feelings of anger, yet if we nurture these thoughts they will eventually resurface to weaken our physical or emotional well-being. Of course anger is a normal human emotion. It's not a sudden flash of anger which harms us so much as the decision to hold a long-term grievance – this only serves to sustain any negative energy associated with the original experience. People say 'I have a right to be angry', which may be true, but they also have the right to be at peace. What price will we pay for our 'right' to be angry? The energy it creates won't provide a state of mind in which we feel nourished and positive about ourselves and our future.

If you feel angry about something in the past you have at least two choices: you can hold onto your anger and the feelings it creates; or you can acknowledge what happened, own your part of it, then let it go and move on. Self-esteem is founded in love; anger is founded in fear. Since we get what we think about, it makes sense to cultivate more love in our thinking than fear. What you give out comes back to you with interest; if you want more love in your life you have to give it out, and you can't give out what your thoughts don't allow you to have.

Unconscious Toxic Emotions

In his personal development lectures, author Dr Wayne Dyer offers the metaphor of the orange to illustrate how we give out what we think about. He asks us what we get if we squeeze an orange; the simple answer is juice. Yet we don't get just any kind of juice – apple or grapefruit juice, for example – for a good reason. Orange juice comes out of an orange because that's what's inside. Similarly when life squeezes us, what comes out is what's inside. If we're holding onto anger and resentment, that's what comes out when we're under pressure.

Dr Dyer also points out that no one has ever died from a snakebite; what kills people is not the bite – it's the poison that remains in their system long after the snake has gone. It's okay to be angry in the short term but nurturing it 'poisons' your life. People who walk around with unresolved anger are rarely having a good time; the thoughts they choose to maintain are causing many problems for them, both physically and emotionally. Choosing to think differently is the fastest way to dissipate these unconsciously stored toxic emotions and one of the most effective ways to do this is through the simple act of forgiveness.

Forgiveness is the fragrance the violet sheds on the heel that has crushed it.
Mark Twain.

When we forgive someone, we don't have to do it for *them*; we can do it for *our own* good. Retraining your unconscious mind to create a healthier sense of self-esteem begins with acts of kindness to oneself, and in the process of forgiving we offer ourselves the ultimate gift of love by removing the toxic negative energy from our system. After all, what has happened has happened; it's in the past and no amount of ruminating will take us back to change those events, but we can change how they affect us in the present. We can choose to remain a prisoner of our darker thoughts or we can set ourselves free. In our willingness to forgive we find the first key to emotional freedom.

It's easy to talk glibly of forgiveness, but it works. Anger and resentment only teach our unconscious mind to sustain a sense of discontent and the ongoing experience of emotional pain.

Holding grievances and anger inside of you is like drinking poison and thinking it will kill your enemy.
Nelson Mandela

Unconscious Self-programming
The seeds of future happiness lie in our current expectations so we must ensure that we guide our thinking towards solutions rather than problems. Life lives up to our expectations, whatever they are, and it's hard to be happy consistently thinking about

what makes us unhappy. It's hard to stop smoking with a mindset that's thinking about cigarettes, because we're setting our filters at an unconscious level to focus on what we don't want. Some people claim they can eat almost anything and never gain an ounce, while others may say, 'Everything I eat goes to my hips.' In each case their unconscious mind has been programmed to support what they believe is true, and they're both right.

We know metabolic rate plays a huge part in the weight gain/loss scenario; however, metabolic rate is unique to each of us and almost entirely influenced by an area of the brain called the hypothalamus. Sometimes referred to as the 'brain's brain', the hypothalamus – about the size of an almond – controls the essential needs of our body, such as the desire to eat. The hypothalamus is directly linked to our nervous system, which in turn is influenced by our thoughts; therefore, people can perhaps influence their weight-loss potential by changing how they think.

It's easy to forget how powerfully we are programming our unconscious mind with our thinking patterns and beliefs. Our unconscious filters react much like a private secretary at the front desk of our awareness, diligently screening the incoming data to determine what should get in and what should stay out. We get a subtle reminder of how this unconscious filtering works when we learn the meaning of a new word and start using it; almost immediately that word seems to show up everywhere – in newspapers, on TV – though of course it's been there all the time; we just didn't see it.

One lady told me she'd started to notice women who were clearly pregnant just as her own pregnancy became obvious. Those other women had always been around, but she'd unconsciously filtered them out because they weren't relevant to her at the time. Many of us will recall having a conversation in a crowded place when we hear our name mentioned in a separate conversation nearby, and we try to listen to both at the same time. We had no idea what the other conversation was about until we heard our name mentioned, yet we must have been able to hear what was said or we couldn't have heard our name. In truth we heard every word, but our unconscious mind decided to delete it.

These examples demonstrate how effectively we unconsciously filter information in or out of our awareness, allowing in only that which matches our deeply held beliefs. This unconscious process causes those with low self-esteem to filter for information which supports their low self-image while at the same time filtering out anything that conflicts with it, but sadly the process isn't confined to people with low self-esteem.

Have you ever noticed that other people's problems seem easy to fix?

They're easy for us to fix because we aren't seeing them through the limitations of the other person's unconscious filters, thus we're better placed to find a solution. People who are good at solving problems have developed a natural ability to change the way they think and unconsciously filter for solutions rather than problems.

Once we understand how unconscious filtering works, the idea that we attract what we think about doesn't seem so strange. But how do we apply this understanding to create a happier life? Knowing what to do isn't much use to us unless we also do what we know. In the next chapters we will learn four powerful strategies to change the way our unconscious mind works, but in order that our current unconscious filters don't undermine our efforts we must develop an awareness that we attract what we think about. Nobody is randomly disposed to think negatively or positively; we've trained our mind to go where it goes, and if we don't like where we find ourselves we must retrain it to take us somewhere else.

The most common way people give up their power is by thinking they don't have any.
Alice Walker

We will begin with a powerful exercise that has been designed to initiate subtle yet effective changes in the way you unconsciously filter information about yourself. We will retrain our unconscious mind to take a positive and solution-focused direction, especially in respect of our core sense of self. Four key steps are gradually introduced over a period of ten days.

Exercise

(Ideally, you should do the first stage of this exercise alone.)

Begin by creating a safe, supportive and stress-free environment.

Make sure you have the time to give to this process without interruptions; disconnect the phone and turn off the television. You may choose a nurturing environment, such as a place of natural beauty, though it doesn't matter where you are as long as you're feeling relaxed.

Step 1

Sit down with a large sheet of paper and write 'Personal Resources' at the top of the page. Now put down the pen and relax for a few moments.

When you're ready, begin to list your qualities and strengths. What are you good at?

Are you a good friend, a caring parent? Do you have a natural skill of some kind? Are you a good listener? Do you seem to have a natural ability to help others? Perhaps you're a great cook.

Write down whatever shows up in your mind, freely exploring any qualities you may have.

At this point your internal voice may interfere, suggesting you should be careful what you write in case someone sees it and thinks you're big-headed. But remember that no one else will ever see this piece of paper but you.

Eventually, you won't be able to think of anything else to

write. Here the magic really begins. Whether your list is long or short, fold it neatly and put it somewhere on your person – perhaps in your pocket or purse – but the list *must* stay with you for the next ten days.

When you change your clothes, transfer the list to your fresh clothes; when you go to bed, put the list close to you where you will see it when you wake up. (If you put it under the pillow, do remember it's there!)

This exercise is asking your mind to initiate an unconscious rather than a conscious search for positive information about yourself, and as long as the list remains on your person your unconscious mind will continue its search. It's like clicking the 'search' button on your computer but with greater effect.

Over the next ten days, your list begins to lengthen as your unconscious mind reminds you of the personal qualities you have been filtering out for years. Fortunately, this requires no conscious effort on your part. Your unconscious mind will effortlessly deliver the relevant information into the 'mailbox' of your conscious awareness.

Step 2

On day five, choose two people who know and care about you, and whom you respect. Ask each person, separately, what in their opinion are your strengths and talents. Other people can have a much clearer view of our qualities than we do because they see us without the self-limiting filters we impose on ourselves. If you have low self-esteem, you probably have several positive attributes that your internal filters have been trained to ignore and now you just don't see them. (Remember how easy it was to look at a sentence and fail to see how many Fs it contained?)

You must now add anything these people tell you to your list – as long as it's positive. You *cannot* veto what they tell you. Over the years, your unconscious mind has interfered with any attempt to recognize your strengths, so that when someone compliments you, you regard it as nothing but flattery. To overcome this, write down anything positive you hear about yourself.

Step 3

Gradually, your unconscious filters begin to focus on your qualities rather than your perceived limitations. Increase the impact of this by reviewing your list each night just before you go to sleep. Research has demonstrated that our mind is powerfully influenced by what we look at in the hour before we sleep; it will review this material by as much as five times more than anything else we did that day – an excellent reason to be mindful of what we watch or think before we go to bed!

As you review your list just before going to sleep, see if you can remember the last time you demonstrated one of these qualities. Bring this memory back into your mind as vividly as you can and notice what it feels like to remember it again; what else can you hear and see as you do this?

Now put your list in a safe place by your bed. As you fall asleep, consider where and when you might demonstrate any one of these qualities again in the near future.

Summary
1. Write a list of your personal resources and qualities.
2. Ask at least two other people to tell you what they think you are good at.
3. Review your list right before you sleep each night and fully associate it into the memory.

This exercise empowers your unconscious mind to search for positive information about yourself and changes the way your unconscious filters operate. Once established, these new directional thinking patterns can be easily reinforced or topped up to ensure that any old negative thinking patterns don't resurface.

Not to be cheered by praise, nor grieved by blame, but to know thoroughly one's own virtues and powers. These are the characteristics of excellence.
Saskya Pandita (1182–1252)

We are encouraged to think about what we put into our body yet we are rarely taught to think about what we blithely allow to filter into our mind.What Are We Letting In?

Low self-esteem encourages a subliminal sense of vulnerability, therefore it's important to avoid anything which supports it. The media is awash with reports of violent crime or health scares, all confirming our fears that we may be at risk. What we read and watch unconsciously programs us, so we can increase our self-worth simply by raising our awareness of what we are exposing ourselves to on a regular basis, particularly negative influences. Although we live in an age of advanced communication systems that provide a constant flow of information into our lives, we can nevertheless decide to be more discerning about what we allow in. What will empower or nourish us? What might initiate unconscious patterns of negativity?

Our unconscious mind can't tell the difference between a real event and a vividly imagined one, so watching a violent movie is fraught with problems. Watching news on television may seem innocuous but the content affects us subliminally. Since 'no news is good news', we are exposed to perhaps an hour of upsetting information. Consciously we realize these stories are about other people, but they have a powerful effect on our system at an unconscious level.

I'm not suggesting that you stop watching the news or any other program, but that you think about what you are watching, when you watch it, and the potential it has to influence the directional flow of your unconscious mind.

A Hard Day's Night

In the UK there's a late-night television program about unsolved crimes, which shows realistic and often violent reconstructions of these events. At a conscious level, viewers know these are reconstructions, but unconsciously it's difficult to be unaffected. As this fear fest ends, the presenter looks sympathetically into the camera and invites the viewers to 'try not to worry, and don't have sleepless nights'. She might as well say, 'Don't think of a pink elephant.'

The presenter suggests we consciously prevent this information from filtering into our mind while we sleep, but we're unconscious when we sleep, so by definition we're unable to influence our dreams. Asking us to remove pre-set visualizations from our unconscious mind just before we fall asleep is like asking a drowning man not to sink. Staying afloat is possible *if* you know how to swim, but while many people can swim, few know how to interrupt unconscious patterns once they're established.

You may not have sleepless nights after exposing your mind to late-night visualizations of fear and negativity, but your unconscious mind will replay what you've just seen more than anything else that day. Is this really the kind of subliminal conditioning you want in your mind before you go to bed?

We either make ourselves miserable, or we make ourselves strong. The amount of work in either case is exactly the same.
Carlos Casteneda

We all have to think – we can't opt out of the process – and if it's true that we attract what we think about, perhaps we should learn to create thinking habits which nourish and empower us rather than those that limit us, especially since one requires no more effort than the other.

Quick Start: Resources

Three small daily challenges

We have spent years training our mind to move automatically in the direction it currently takes. Choose one of the following three steps to begin the process of automatic directional change:

1. Take a short media break. Stop listening to the news or reading newspapers for 24 hours.
2. You can't attract solutions by thinking of problems, so spend two minutes twice a day asking yourself what you can feel proud of, or grateful for, in your life.
3. Find one new way each day to treat yourself with love and kindness, and that energy will begin to attract people into your life who will treat you the same way.

5

Imagine (I)

Brain researchers estimate that your unconscious database outweighs the conscious by a ratio exceeding ten million to one. This database is the source of your hidden natural genius. In other words, a part of you is much smarter than you are. The wise people regularly consult that smart part.

Michael J. Gelb, author of *How to Think Like Leonardo da Vinci*

'I really want to quit, but to be honest I just can't see it happening.'

Dan's face tightened as he took another tug of his cigarette, then relaxed as he blew the wisp of grey smoke towards the yellowed ceiling of the pub. He'd spent the last ten minutes telling me about his latest attempt to stop smoking; at least three other attempts that I knew of had all ended the same way. Dan is a bright guy who knows what he wants: to stop smoking. But he can't seem to make it happen despite trying everything he can think of, and it's driving him nuts with frustration. He says he has all the motivating factors in place for quitting: knowledge of the health benefits, the financial advantage, and willpower. Yet he just can't seem to quit. Why?

However One essential ingredient for change was missing from Dan's list and he'd just told me what it was.

He couldn't see it happening.

He was not unusual; I'd heard this many times before from people who had tried unsuccessfully to create change in their life. Millions all over the world right now are beginning similar journeys. Someone somewhere has just decided to stop smoking, lose weight, or increase their self-confidence. Some will succeed and some will fail, and almost everyone who fails has one important thing in common: they all struggle to create an internal picture of themselves experiencing the outcome they want. Some of them, like Dan, will indicate this without fully realizing what they're saying.

If we can't see it in our mind to begin with, we're unlikely to see it anywhere else later on. Conversely we can plant the seeds of our future success by seeing ourselves in the changes we want, primarily because our unconscious mind will attract whatever we consistently think about. These internal pictures have the power to lift or deplete us, both physically and emotionally.

Think back to the lady in Chapter 2 who lifted the car that was crushing her granddaughter: what kind of mental imagery was she running in order to achieve that feat? The painful images that flashed across her mind triggered a process that instantly allowed her to access physical strength far beyond what she believed possible. This is why sports psychologists use visualization exercises to raise the physical capacity of athletes; they understand that the mind is not merely an equal partner in the business of improved physical performance but the majority shareholder, and that we can all run faster, jump higher and feel stronger by repeatedly playing images of the outcomes we want.

If you have never used imagery to improve your physical performance, try the following simple exercise, and experience how it works for yourself.

Exercise

Place your thumb and forefinger together to form a circle, then invite a friend to hook their first and second fingers through the circle and try to pull your thumb and finger apart.

Try as hard as you can to resist and keep the circle of thumb and forefinger together.

Unless your friend has very little strength they'll quickly succeed in separating your fingers.

Now relax for a moment. You're going to try the same thing again, but this time, you will prepare yourself differently:

When you're relaxed, close your eyes and place your thumb and forefinger gently together, picturing yourself holding the most beautiful butterfly in the world between your thumb and finger. You mustn't hold it too tightly or you'll kill it; but you must hold it firmly enough to stop it flying away.

Stay relaxed, and keep your eyes closed with the image of the butterfly in your mind. When you feel you have a clear picture, invite your friend to separate your fingers again using the same process as before. But this time, with your eyes closed and the image of the butterfly in your mind, silently repeat to yourself, 'Hold onto this butterfly.'

If your internal image is strong, your friend will find it much harder to open your fingers; if it's very strong, they'll be unable to open them no matter how hard they try.

Now, if it's possible to increase the strength in your fingers simply by holding an image in your mind, what kind of powerful changes could be initiated by practicing a specific visualization for a week or two?

* * *

Our thoughts powerfully influence the programs of our unconscious mind and we must be mindful that we will attract what we think about. When we worry, we see fear-based images that powerfully influence our unconscious mind. But worrying isn't an effective way to deal with our problems; if it was, we could just sit down and worry till our problems disappeared!

There is so much in the world for us all if we only have eyes to see it, and the heart to love it, and the hand to gather it to ourselves.
Lucy Maud Montgomery (1874–1942)

In fact in most cases, worrying makes things worse since it blocks the natural flow of solution-focused energy and instead creates a mental state in which solutions seem to become invisible. Most people realize it's harder to find a solution by worrying about the problem but they continue to worry, creating images of what they don't want and playing them over and over like a film in their mind.

An example of this can be seen on most commercial airline flights. Just as the plane takes off, one of the passengers tightly grips the arm of his seat, looking extremely worried. His look of fear is an external expression of the film he's watching in his mind, showing air disasters in vivid widescreen Technicolor and surround sound. The other passengers are each playing their own private internal film, resulting in a wide variety of emotional outcomes. Some may be anticipating a perfect vacation in which everything goes right, while others run images of a trip where everything possible goes wrong. Happily, we can choose what we want to watch.

In La Jolla, Southern California, people swim around a large circuit marked out by buoys in the bay. You need to be a strong swimmer to complete a couple of laps, because after all, this isn't a leisure center but the ocean. Every morning several people show up to swim circuits, yet they all seem unperturbed by one piece of relevant information: there are huge sharks in the water beneath them. A local lifeguard explained this to me one summer morning as we stood together watching the swimmers moving slowly through the water; apparently the bay provides a perfect environment for sharks to breed and raise their young. Seeing the look of horror on my face, he quickly assured me that the swimmers would be fine – the sharks never bothered anyone and it was perfectly safe.

I couldn't believe that anyone could happily swim in the ocean when large sharks were right beneath them. The lifeguard smiled at my disbelief and explained that not only was it true but it was also common local knowledge – most of the swimmers in the bay knew it yet continued to swim, seemingly unaffected.

This raises an interesting question: How do these people stay in the water knowing huge sharks are in there with them?

It's easy: they don't visualize shark attacks while they're swimming. If they did, it would be almost impossible for them to continue.

Anyone who saw the movie *Jaws* may recall seeing the legs of a swimmer treading water from the shark's perspective below. Although this image was pure Hollywood fiction, it created enough fear to stop many people swimming in the ocean for years afterwards. We might still hear *that soundtrack* playing in our mind when we swim a little too far out from the beach, and if those images flood back into our mind we'll find it difficult to remain in the water.

The fear-based pictures of our imagination can leave us feeling vulnerable and frightened but the process works just as effectively in reverse. By replacing problematic thinking habits with solution-focused images we can empower resources we never thought possible; all we need do is change our internal film, once we understand how to work the projector.

Success is a state of mind, if you want success, start seeing yourself as a success.
Dr Joyce Brothers

Few things can influence our unconscious mind as powerfully as pictures.If we consistently visualize an image of ourselves in an experience that is different from the one we currently have, we create a sense of unease since our unconscious mind can't tell the difference between what is really happening to us and what is imagined. This leads to a form of cognitive dissonance – an underlying feeling of psychological unease experienced by trying to hold two contradictory ideas at the same time.

The fable of 'The Fox and the Grapes' by Aesop (ca. 620–564 BC) is often cited as a good portrayal of cognitive dissonance. In the fable a thirsty fox sees a juicy bunch of ripe grapes hanging from a vine; thinking this is just what he needs to quench his thirst, he tries repeatedly to leap up and snatch them, only to fail each time. Eventually the fox gives up, telling himself as he walks away that the grapes would have been useless anyway as they were probably unripe.

This provides a good example of justifying to yourself why you don't want what you can't have. People who smoke when they want to quit know that smoking causes ill health and even death, yet they continue to smoke. Like anyone else, they want to live long and healthy lives yet their smoking habit diminishes the likelihood of them doing so. This conflict between their behavior and beliefs creates cognitive dissonance – a sense that something is wrong but they're not sure what. This feeling of unrest continues to niggle away in their unconscious mind until it is resolved by removing one of the conflicting ideas.

A smoker must either quit smoking or invent a story to justify his continued conflicting behavior. He may tell himself that only a small percentage of smokers actually die from smoking, therefore the chances of staying healthy are reasonably good. The story doesn't have to be true or even logical, just plausible enough to allow him to continue smoking. The other way to resolve the cognitive dissonance, of course, is to stop smoking.

We can also create the same sense of unease by holding two conflicting images in our mind at the same time. This is what happens when we practice a visualization exercise over a period of time; we run pictures in our mind of what we want, while simultaneously experiencing what we have; our unconscious mind struggles to distinguish what we imagine from what is real and becomes confused.

We might experience a mild form of this visual conflict when we visit someone who has recently remodeled their home. If we are impressed, we unconsciously create comparisons with where we live; then when we get home, we say 'We should redecorate this place.' Our home was just fine when we left it earlier, but now we have a picture of something better, and these two conflicting images begin to influence our unconscious mind. This psychological conflict is the driving force behind most sales pitches and the principle reason why new housing developments include a 'show home'. Fortunately, our unconscious mind is programmed to resolve this kind of conflict soon after it arises; it's as if we pass a threshold of tolerance which triggers our unconscious mind to resolve the situation. This automatic ability is a powerful tool in the process of change.

The greatest danger for most of us is not that our aim is too high and we miss it, but that it is too low and we achieve it.
Michelangelo

As we have seen, if we visualize an outcome that is clearly different from the one we currently have, there are only two ways to resolve the tension: either we stop visualizing what we want or we find a way to turn it into a reality. In short, we must either *get* it or *forget* it. If we forget it, the tension created by the visualization quickly disappears along with the prospect of making it a reality. This may be the case with people who say they know what they want but can't see it happening.

However, if we continue to practice the visualization intentionally, our unconscious mind explores the other option: turning our visualization into a reality. This process creates improved results in every area of life and relationships, and is used by many successful people all over the world. Watch Olympic athletes as they prepare to compete in a final event. Are they mindlessly strolling around? Not at all. They can see an internal video that they've watched a thousand times before and it plays out the same way every time: they see themselves performing at the highest level of their ability, achieving the outcome they want. Their visualization can't guarantee success but it significantly improves their chances.

I never hit a shot, not even in practice, without seeing a very sharp, in-focus picture of it in my head.
Jack Nicklaus

We know that our mind attracts what we think about, so if we mentally rehearse the changes we want, we provide it with a target at which to direct its subliminal attention. Seeing internal pictures of ourselves in the outcomes we want is one of the most influential habits we could ever cultivate in our desire for change.

Exercise

(This is best done while standing up.)

Imagine a circle on the ground in front of you. Notice the size and colour of the circle. Picture the circle in vivid color, glowing with positive energy.

When you are ready, recall a time in the past when you felt confident or very happy.

Now imagine that confident/happy 'you' standing in the circle in front of you.

What do you look like when you are more confident/happy?

How can you tell the person in the circle is confident/happy?

Is it the way they speak? Are they smiling? Or is something else happening?

What kind of positive energy is flowing around them in the circle – what color is it?

As you notice these things, step into the circle and let this same energy surround you.

Experience what it's like to be this person again; notice where the feeling is strongest.

When you sense this positive energy is reaching its height, step out of the circle.

Look back and see the circle filled with the positive energy you experienced there.

Now think of a future situation when it could be useful to have that positive energy again. Imagine that future situation. What do you see around you in the moments just before you want to have this positive energy back again? You may hear your name spoken, or see a particular person or the inside of a room.

As the image grows stronger, step into your circle and feel its positive energy again.

When you are ready to do so, step out of the circle.

You now have a powerful resource with which to increase your confidence in any situation. By imagining your circle on the floor in front of you and then stepping into the circle when the positive energy is at its highest point, confidence will effortlessly flow through you again.

This exercise pre-programs your unconscious mind to associate positive energy with an imagined future event. The more you practice, the stronger will become the association.

Try it again without using the instructions.

Some people have problems remembering a time when they felt confident. They may not be sure what it looks, sounds, and feels like. In this case, imagine someone else standing in the circle who clearly is confident. It needn't be someone you know; it can even be a fictional character from a movie so long as it's someone who demonstrates the emotion you want to experience; it's also a good idea to pick someone you respect or admire.

This simple exercise illustrates how quickly we can train our unconscious mind to associate a specific emotion such as confidence with a visual trigger.

* * *

The idea that we can create a better future by visualizing it in our present may seem just a little too abstract to those who have been taught to believe only what they can see. Of course we can't see someone's unconscious mind being influenced by the images it consistently sees, but we do see the legacy of those images reflected in the kind of life they live. Many people nowadays understand the power of imagery to create change, but relatively few regularly use the skills of creative visualization. The obstacle isn't a lack of understanding or skill but a lack of belief. Visualization without belief is a waste of time and the fast track to greater unhappiness. Just imagining change isn't enough to make it happen; you also have to believe in it.

You can be anything you want to be, if only you believe with sufficient conviction and act in accordance with your faith, for whatever the mind can conceive and believe, the mind can achieve.
Napoleon Hill, author of *Think and Grow Rich*

The most convincing evidence in support of visualization is gained from practice. Those who use these skills to create change in their lives have actually experienced the power of their imagination and need no further evidence. Nothing can replace first-hand experience.

Now that we understand how and why pictures can have such a great impact on us, we need the skill to apply it. In the following pages we will discover three extremely effective ways to re-program our unconscious mind towards positive and lasting change and we'll learn faster if we stay relaxed. Visualizing what we want is an excellent way to create what we want, but the process must be effortless; any conscious attempt to force or hurry the outcome blocks our natural flow of unconscious energy and does more harm than good. Likewise, becoming tense or stressed decreases our ability to succeed, so we must learn to relax in our practice and trust the power of our unconscious mind to handle the details.

We begin by learning a simple visualization we can practice anytime, anywhere.

Quick Start: Resources

Beginning with the end

Spend a few minutes today imagining how you would look if you felt more confident.

If that seems too difficult, think of someone you know and like who is confident and imagine what it would feel like to be like them.

See this internal picture as often and in as much detail as possible.

As you imagine yourself in this confident state of mind, ask any of the following questions:

1. What does this feel like?
2. When have I felt like this before?
3. What was I doing last time I felt like this?
4. Where was I the last time I felt like this?
5. Where might it be helpful to feel like this in future?

6

Imagine (II)

If we did all the things we were capable of doing, we would literally astound ourselves.
Thomas Edison

Visualization is an extremely effective way to rewrite the program of the unconscious mind and thereby control our quality of life, so it makes sense to learn this skill. Fortunately, there isn't much to learn because we're already experts. You've been using visualization to influence your emotions all your life, mostly without realizing it. When you look forward to a pleasant event, you produce internal pictures that create a shift in your state of mind; similarly when you worry about something, you imagine pictures of an outcome you don't want, and affect your emotions negatively. However, we need to understand how to refine this natural ability and redirect it to help us achieve our goals.

Few people fully realize the power they have to influence their unconscious mind with pictures yet this can become our most effective tool for transformation. The key to using these skills successfully lies in you knowing what you want, then picturing it clearly as an outcome that has *already happened*. You don't have to know how it will happen (your unconscious mind will handle those details for you); you only need to see it as something that has already taken place. If you want more self-confidence, you start by picturing what a confident 'you' would look like. You don't have to *be* confident; you only need to see what you will look like when you are.

Personal change is a journey of transformation, from where

you are now to where you'd rather be, and one of the principle reasons people find this hard is that they get bogged down trying to figure out how to get from one place to the other. Visualizing what you want as if it has already happened takes your attention away from the *how* part of the change process and places it instead on the result. In this way, you stimulate your subliminal resources, causing the *how* to become transparently clear to you. How you get from A to B is less important than your ability to imagine what B will be like when you get there.

Before we learn how to use our first simple visualization, consider what changes you want to create in your life. What springs quickly to mind? What would be most helpful to you right now? More self-esteem and confidence? Less anxiety?

Think about why it would be helpful to have these changes in your life now. What you would do differently as a result? How would your life change – how would *you* change?

What would be possible in your life if you make these changes now? Now imagine that you can travel forwards in time and see yourself months or years from now in a future when you have all these changes in your life, then consider the following two questions:

1. As you look at that happier future 'you', how do you know you have changed?
2. What does the future 'you' do differently?

Is it the way they move, or speak? Is it how they look –are they dressed differently? ? What is different?

Notice as many details as you can that make it obvious that the changes you desire have taken place. Take as long as you like over this.

How can you tell this future 'you' is more confident and happy? Is it a feeling you get when you look at the picture? If so, what kind of feelingis that??

You should now have a future-based image in which you are happier and more confident; it may not be too clear at first but the images will quickly improve as you get more comfortable with them. Although these pictures exist only in your imagination for now, the influence they will have on your unconscious mind will eventually change you.

The future belongs to those who believe in the beauty of their dreams.
Eleanor Roosevelt

Let's develop all this a little further.

We're going to learn a simple visualization to improve self-confidence, though it could be adapted to support change of any kind. Before you try it, you may find it helpful to read through the exercise a few times, to reduce any need to keep referring back to the details. There is also find a five-step summary of this first exercise towards the end of the chapter, for those who prefer to take their information in bigger chunks.

To begin, find a safe and nurturing environment, and turn off your phone, radio and TV. Make yourself comfortable, sitting, standing, or even lying – whatever works for you.

You may also find it helpful to 'center' yourself before you practice, as this will relax you, make it easier to imagine the changes you want, and improve the quality of your results. A simple centering strategy is to place your attention on your breath (see the breathing techniques in Chapter 9 for further examples).

Sit comfortably and when you are ready, simply observe the steady movement of your breath as it flows effortlessly in and out of your body.

Don't try to change your breathing pattern in any way; simply relax and allow yourself to breathe normally and easily. Follow the flow of each out-breath to its limit and then pay attention to the flow of new air as your lungs begin to gently refill themselves.

Imagine any worries or anxieties leaving you with each out-breath.

Imagine an energy of calmness and peace entering your body with each in-breath.

Notice what 'color' the in-breath is and whether it feels cool or warm as it enters your body.

Notice what the out-breath is like as it carries away any stress and tension from within.

Does it have a color? Is it warm or cool?

Do nothing more than this for the next two or three minutes, remaining relaxed. If a thought pops into your mind, simply release it and return your attention to your breath.

Then read through the following exercise before starting.

Exercise

Remember how you will be when you have made the changes you desire. Imagine a future in which you are living your life exactly as you would like to be.

See these pictures of yourself as if you are watching a film on a screen in your mind.

Notice how far in front of you the screen is.

What do you notice about the other 'you' in the film? What makes it obvious they are confident and self-assured?

What else?

As you look at that picture, notice if there is any color in it. Put color into it, and if it has color already, turn it up.

Make your picture brighter.

Turn the sound on. If it's already on, make it louder.

Make the picture bigger. Now make it life-size.

Imagine walking towards the picture, and pause when you can feel its positive energy. Wait there until you can really feel that positive energy radiating out from the picture.

Move closer to the screen and, when you are ready, step into the picture and try it on like a coat that completely surrounds you. Sense the positive energy flowing through you.

Notice what happens as you fully relax into this energy.

What word best describes this positive experience to you? Choose a word or expression that sums up your emotions now.

Any positive word that comes to mind is provided by your unconscious mind as an audio connection between the positive emotions you are feeling and the images you can see.

Keep this word in your thoughts and use it each time you think about your visualization.

When you are ready to finish the visualization, bring your attention gently back to the space around you, bringing with you any new discoveries you may have experienced during the course of the exercise.

You now have a memory pathway to an emotional experience that is both powerful and positive, and a password to help you establish it more easily. The more you can experience such images, the more your unconscious mind will notice the dissonance between the way you are now and the way you imagine yourself to be in the visualization. This is one of the most effective ways to create change in your life, and as you become more familiar with the practice you'll find that you are able to adjust and refine your internal pictures to suit your changing needs with ease.

We can summarize what we've done here in five key stages:

1. We began by centering ourselves, which helps us to access our most resourceful state.
2. We imagined a future scenario in which we had already achieved the changes we want.
3. We altered our internal pictures by increasing the color, size, brightness and sound.
4. We got into the picture, *fully associating* our senses with every aspect of the experience.

5. We created an audio trigger between the positive emotions and the images in our mind.

You just give folks a key, and they can open their own locks.
Robert McCammon

If we explore these key points, we will see how such a seemingly simple process can work so effectively. Step 1 is self-evident since we perform at a higher level when we feel good about ourselves rather than when we feel stressed or under pressure.

In Step 2 we created an image of how we want to be in the future and viewed it from an external perspective just as we might watch a movie on a screen. All we have at this point is a standard visualization of what we want; it's effective but it lacks the magic we're about to introduce in Step 3. Here we altered the sub-modalities: we turned up the brightness, increased the color and sound, and made the picture bigger. These changes made your experience of the visualization increasingly realistic, and your unconscious mind, which can't tell the difference between what is real and imagined, responded as if it was all happening for real.

Step 4 provides what is possibly the most powerful impact of all on our unconscious mind by altering our perceptual position from dissociated to associated. By stepping into the image in our mind, we significantly increase all the associated positive emotions that it brings, and as these positive emotions reached their height we introduced a word (in Step 5) to provide a trigger for the positive emotions of the visualization. If we introduce that word at exactly the same point each time we practice the visualization, our unconscious mind will quickly create a shortcut from the word to the positive emotion, in the same way as we might establish a shortcut on our computer desktop.

Why does it matter *how* we see these images in our mind?

It matters because altering your imagined pictures in this way allows you to experience your desired changes *here in the present moment*; this will affect you powerfully because your unconscious mind is influenced more by what is happening *now* than what might happen in the future. Whenever we think about our future, we must invent the pictures we see since they obviously haven't happened yet, whereas we remember our past as memories, but whether we think about the future or the past, we do so from either an internal or an external perspective. We refer to this respectively as 'associated' or 'dissociated' imagery. 'Associated' means we view the experience from within, when the picture surrounds us. If you stop reading and look up, you'll see whatever is in your field of vision but you won't be able to see what is behind you without turning to look; therefore it could be said that you are associated or *in* that experience. By contrast, if you experienced yourself from an external viewpoint (much as you might watch a film of yourself on a TV screen), you'd be able to see what was happening behind you because you'd be looking from an external viewpoint. In this case we could say you were 'dissociated' from what you see and therefore *out* of the picture.

Shifting our perception of an event from associated to dissociated, and vice versa, is an effective way to gain more control over how it affects us emotionally, though it isn't our only option. We can further increase or decrease the emotional impact of any imagined event by increasing or decreasing the sub-modalities as in the above exercise. One slight alteration in how you remember or anticipate things can make a huge difference to your happiness and quality of life. When we associate into an image, the related emotions are greatly enhanced and affect us much more; when we dissociate from it, the reverse happens – the respective emotions affect us less. Dissociating from painful memories won't entirely remove their emotional impact but will diminish it significantly, perhaps by half as much as when you fully associate into it.

Consider the implications of this for a moment:

- Associated (*in the picture*) increases the emotional impact of what you are picturing.

- Dissociated (*out of the picture*) decreases the emotional impact of what you are picturing.

Consider what kind of life experience you would have if every time you remembered an unpleasant event you fully associated into it, increasing the sound, color and brightness. What if you tried to imagine a more positive future, but saw it from an external perspective as a small black-and-white picture without any sound?

Would that be a useful or helpful thing to do?

Of course not, yet many people just think about their lives in their own unique way and then wonder why they find it so difficult to create positive change and a happier future. But here we have a simple yet valuable tool for change: enhancing the effects of a positive thought by experiencing it in an associated way, and reducing the effects of an unpleasant memory by experiencing it as an external image. Simply raising your awareness of these two factors can help you to think in a more energizing way while diminishing the influence of painful memories.

Whatever you have experienced in your life is carved in stone.
But today ... at this very moment ... you have the power to make the
shift, from where you are to where you want to be.
davidji

We all create different types of internal imagery for our memories or our pictures of the future: some of us see them in black and white, while others include color but not sound; some have sound and color but see a still frame rather than a rolling film. These individual differences are unlikely to become a hot topic of conversation because most of us live our entire lives without once thinking about it. We remain unaware of the power of our imagination.

The way we see things also influences our level of self-esteem, working for us or against us. The following five-step formula provides an interesting example of how this operates.

Exercise

Think of a past experience which makes you feel *slightly* uncomfortable. Don't choose the most unpleasant event that ever happened, but something that makes you feel a bit flat whenever you remember it.

When you have thought about that memory for a few moments, try these steps:

1. Step out of the memory and see it as a picture on a screen in front of you.
2. Watch the color drain out of it until it becomes a black-and-white picture.
3. Make the picture less sharp and slightly out of focus.
4. Turn the brightness down – in fact, make it quite dull – and turn the sound right down or off.
5. Rapidly minimize the picture in size until it's small enough to fit on a cell-phone screen.

What happened to the way you experienced this memory when you changed the way you viewed it?

* * *

We all have memories – some happy, some sad – though the emotional impact is determined more by *how* we remember than *what* we remember. Some painful memories keep us feeling stuck; we find it hard to put them in the past where they belong. The good news is that we are not at their mercy; we have power over the way they affect us. Obviously, we cannot go back in time and change the past, but we can change the way we view the past and so change the emotions it produces in the present.

That painful event may have happened a long time ago in our dim and distant past, but if we view it from an associated perspective and increase all the sub-modalities it will have a very negative and debilitating effect – almost as upsetting as if it were happening again – and that would be a poor strategy for change since it allows our past to run our future. Again the principle works equally well the other way: when we imagine a happier future we should increase the image's color, sound, and size, and step into it, fully associating into its positive energy and thereby maximizing its impact.

The greatest achievement was at first and for a time only a dream.
James Allen

It is important to remember that our unconscious mind can't tell the difference between what is real and what is imagined, therefore it responds to every visualization as if it were real. If someone with low self-confidence visualizes themselves being confident, the images create cognitive dissonance because they conflict with the person's current sense of self, and their unconscious mind cannot tell which image is real. If they continue that visualization, their unconscious mind moves to resolve the conflict caused by it – in one of only two ways. The person either stops using the visualization or else alters the way they feel about themselves, until they resemble the confident image. Since our sense of self is empowered unconsciously, this change happens naturally.

This sounds very simple – because it is! People with high self-esteem don't use complicated strategies to sustain their positive self-image; it happens effortlessly, because their sense of self is created and sustained unconsciously. If you have developed low self-esteem over time, training your unconscious mind to hold a negative sense of self, you can reverse this unconscious conditioning and attract abundance into of your life simply by seeing pictures of yourself in the future you want. We attract what we think about, therefore it is in our best interest to cultivate thoughts about the future we want rather than the problems we may currently have. In short, we must begin with the end in mind.

Hope stirs imagination and imagination stirs change.

Five-Step 'Big Chunk' Version of a Confidence Visualization

1. Imagine what you will look like when you are more confident.
2. Notice as many things as you can about this image.
3. Make the image brighter and turn the sound and the color up.
4. Make the picture bigger; make it life-size.
5. Step into the picture and let it surround you.

Getting comfortable with this five-step summary may make it easier for you to practice the more detailed version given earlier. Either way, it is the amount of time and commitment you give to your practice which brings success.

When and how often should you practice a visualization?

It's entirely up to the individual, but the more often you show your unconscious mind images of what you want, the more powerfully it will be affected. Personally, I think there are two key times in each day when your practice will have the greatest impact: first thing in the morning, when your mind is in the alpha state and open to positive conditioning; and, perhaps most importantly, last thing at night right before you go to sleep.

Outside of this, there is no set limit to how often you practice in any 24-hour period.

Several remarkable things happen once you get into the habit of seeing yourself in the changes you want. Chance meetings and seemingly coincidental events begin to take place with surprising frequency, and opportunities arise in unlikely circumstances. When you cultivate these skills consistently, it may start to feel like some universal intelligence is aware of what you are trying to do and is moving to help and support you. However, remember that we must take the first step ourselves in order to empower this energy of change.

In the moment one definitely commits oneself, then Providence moves too. All sorts of things occur to help us that would never otherwise have occurred, unforeseen incidents, chance meetings, and material assistance, which no man could have dreamed would come his way.

Johann Wolfgang von Goethe

Our unconscious mind, this powerful tool for change, comes to us as standard equipment at birth but with no user's guide, so we must learn to harness and apply its resources to create and sustain the life we want. No one else can do this for us; we alone have to direct it by showing it what we want.

We have gained the first of three effective tools to re-program our unconscious mind. These are not difficult skills and will pay us a handsome return on our investment of time and effort. Your challenge is to 'begin with the end in mind' and practice one of the exercises in this chapter at least twice a day for 30 days. Trust in the power of your unconscious mind to take care of the *how* part of the transformation.

The next step in our journey reveals the second of our tools for change: language direction awareness. Contrary to the popular expression, talk is not cheap; in fact, as we shall discover, we may already be paying an emotional price for the words we consistently hear.

Quick Start: Resources

Looking back down the road you have traveled

Imagine yourself in a future situation where you feel more confident.

Turn up the color, sound and brightness.

Step into the image and fully associate into its positive energy.

Allow this positive feeling a few moments to grow stronger.

When you feel fully associated into this experience, imagine you are looking back down the passage of time to this moment in the present.

As you look back at the path you have successfully traveled to this state of unconscious confidence, answer the following three questions:

1. What was the most helpful thing you did?
2. How and when did you do it?
3. What help or advice could you now offer someone trying to achieve this goal?

You may notice some key moments that were particularly important to you along the way.

7

Language Direction Awareness

Life is not a static thing. The only people who don't change their minds are incompetents in asylums who can't, and those in cemeteries.

Everett Dirksen

Research shows that 55% of human communication is non-verbal and takes the form of body language, 38% is carried by the tone of our voice, and only 7% of our meaning is conveyed by the actual words we speak. Nevertheless, language exerts a powerful emotional influence; it can inspire us beyond the confines of our perceived limitations, igniting hope and optimism in the ashes of frustration and failure. The right words empower us, while the wrong ones leave us disheartened as we sense our positive energy draining away.

In this chapter we explore the hidden potential of words and the critical role language plays in determining our self-esteem and happiness. Talk may indeed be cheap, but the words we use may turn out to be priceless.

People are constantly trying to create personal change of some kind – to stop smoking, gain confidence, lose weight – yet most remain unaware that the way they speak makes the difference between success and failure. A smoker may try many different approaches to solve his problem but fail to realize that he is just as influenced by what he consistently says as by what he does.

When re-programming our unconscious mind, what we see is more powerful than what we hear, yet words generate pictures, so we can change what we see by changing how we speak. Words direct our unconscious mind to establish automatic tendencies towards a positive or negative view of the world. Since we were not born with either view, it seems we have unconsciously programmed ourselves one way or the other. If we unconsciously hold a low sense of self-worth, it will show up in the way we speak, which in turn will confirm our low self-worth to our unconscious mind. This creates a downward cycle of communication in which one factor continuously supports the negative energy of the other. If we allow this to take root, we begin filtering for any information that confirms our negative sense of self, while filtering out anything which contradicts it; once in place, this habit of self-deprecation can be hard to break.

Habit is habit and not to be flung out of the window by any man, but coaxed downstairs one step at a time.
Mark Twain

Unfortunately, our culture cultivates low self-esteem by teaching us to be modest, to play down our good qualities so we don't appear conceited. In so doing, we may overcompensate and train ourselves to be uncomfortable with the very idea of self-worth. Being obnoxiously boastful is one thing; failing to acknowledge our true self-worth is another; and while trying to avoid one, we mustn't fall under the spell of the other. If people give us compliments or praise, we should receive it without discomfort or the desire to deflect it. There's a useful little phrase you can practice saying if you're lost for words after a compliment: 'Thank you'.

Thanking people who offer you praise or a compliment is a simple way to begin using language to create change, because your unconscious mind is listening to everything you say and hear, and responses from you that devalue the praise you have been given train it to disregard any future acknowledgments of your value. This is why we must avoid speaking in a way that identifies our problems with who we are, for example saying, 'I am depressed' or 'I am stressed'. Of course, nothing much is gained by telling ourselves we're happy if we feel depressed – since such denial just creates a sense of repression, leading to greater problems in the long term – but we can use words that honestly describe *how we feel* rather than *who we are*.

Let's explore what happens at an unconscious level when we make the apparently innocent statement, 'I am depressed'. The words 'I am' direct our unconscious mind to associate whatever follows them with our sense of identity; therefore if we claim to *be* depressed, it hears the suggestion that *we are* the malady in question. This may suggest that we need to lose a part of our self in order to be rid of it – an unnatural and difficult task. However, if we speak in a way that describes our experience as just another transient emotion, the effect is much reduced because our unconscious mind doesn't associate such a state of mind with who we are.

In his whole life man achieved nothing so great and so wonderful as when he learned to talk.
Otto Jesperson, Danish philologist

So instead of saying 'I'm depressed', we can simply choose to say 'I'm *feeling* depressed', using language to create a clear distinction between our emotions and our identity. This kind of verbal change should not be confused with emotional denial because we are truthfully acknowledging the way we feel.

Exercise
Make the following statements to yourself, allowing a gap of about ten seconds between each so you can notice how each one affects you:

1. 'I am stressed.'
2. 'I am feeling stressed.'
3. 'I am choosing to feel stressed.'

What did you notice as you paused to consider the effects of each statement in turn?

Perhaps the emotional effect of the word 'stressed' began to diminish. The first statement carries a suggestion to our unconscious mind that we're not just experiencing stress but it's actually a key aspect of who we are. The second makes a clear distinction between who we are and the emotional experience of stress; and the third reminds us at an unconscious level who is calling the shots in allowing the emotion of stress to continue. No one has to 'be' their stress; it's just another emotional response to the circumstances of life – a response we can change through these subtle linguistic alterations.

Let's see how the same process can help someone who may be feeling depressed.

1. 'I am depressed' (subliminally suggests that depression is an aspect of our identity).
2. 'I am feeling depressed' (changes subliminal inference from identity to state of mind).
3. 'I've been doing this depression thing lately' (shifts the malady up to a level of doing).

Statement 3 carries the added benefit of reminding our unconscious mind that we are not in a continuous state of depression; we may do it a lot but we don't do it all the time, since no one could ever be that consistent. Of course, some people seem to be always happy and others always depressed, but in truth our lives consist of both good and bad days; we can't stay fixed at one end of the emotional spectrum for long.

The only truly consistent people on this planet are the dead.
Aldous Huxley

It is much easier to train our unconscious mind to flow in the direction of solutions rather than problems if we learn to speak in a way that dissociates us from our limitations. Negative self-talk is one of the pillars of low self-esteemand can be hard to silence.. Most of us have tried to consciously overcome this kind of destructive internal dialogue at some time and we know from experience that telling ourselves to 'stop talking like that' doesn't work.

One reason why this approach isn't helpful is because t it involves a statement rather than a question. Our unconscious mind seems to disregard statements; if they challenge our present experiences they initiate a strong level of unconscious resistance. Many self-help programs teach the practice of positive affirmations to help build self-esteem, and while these can undoubtedly support us, they are not magic bullets. If they ignore the emotions we are experiencing at the time, they simply create subliminal conflict. 'Fake it till you make it' may be a useful idea in a specific situation, but in the long term we need something stronger. Questions create a stir of a different kind, but we must ask the kind of questions that channel our unconscious mind towards solutions and possibilities; the wrong choice of question only moves us further into our problems and limitations.

If for every time I loved you, words could disappear, then silence, oh yes silence, would be all that you could hear.
Emily Matthews, 'Silence'

Exercise

Ask yourself the following questions, pausing to consider each for at least 30 seconds. Try not to move on to the next question until you have answered the one you are on.

1. What makes me feel unhappy about myself?
2. Why does this make me feel unhappy?

3. How would I prefer to be?
4. What would my life be like if I were 50% happier than I am now?
5. What would I be like if my life was just the way I'd like it to be?

Where did your mind go to consider each question and where did it leave you emotionally? Questions 1 and 2 direct our mind to explore a presenting problem whereas questions 3, 4 and 5 direct our thinking towards solutions and this happens without creating the kind of resistance caused by a conflicting statement. Remember, we're not using these questions to ignore or deny unwanted emotional issues, because that won't work; we're using them to direct our unconscious mind towards solutions.

He who asks questions cannot avoid finding the answers.
African proverb

Every question we ask draws our unconscious mind in a positive or negative direction, potentially keeping us stuck in negative thought patterns. When we feel anxious or upset it seems so easy to ask ourselves the kind of questions that direct our unconscious mind into the problem, and so the cycle of negativity begins. The journey of change will be much easier once we begin to ask questions designed to shift the focus of our unconscious mind towards solutions.

- Questions invite our unconscious mind to explore a specific direction, and since we attract what we think about we must be very careful which questions we ask.

- Statements that conflict with or dismiss how we feel will be challenged or disregarded by our unconscious mind.

The answers lie in the questions. Unfortunately, when most people feel unhappy or depressed, they ask one unhelpful question: 'Why?'

When we ask a 'why' question we invite our unconscious mind to explore all the reasons *why* we have that particular problem. This may seem reasonable, but it obstructs the natural flow of solution-focused thinking. One of the principle ingredients for low self-esteem is a self-deprecating dialogue which leads people to ask 'Why do I speak to myself this way?', inviting themselves to analyze the problem. Our unconscious mind, which cannot tell the difference between what is real or imagined, lists all the reasons why we don't like ourselves and brings our self-esteem even lower than before. Explanations may be helpful but don't provide a sustainable solution. Given the choice between knowing why you have low self-esteem and being able quickly and permanently to increase it, which option would you choose? No doubt, you'd choose a solution over an explanation every time. In addition, searching for an explanation almost always results in merely finding a *label*, so is often a waste of time and resources.

Words form the thread on which we string our experiences.
Aldous Huxley

It is easy to develop the habit of asking solution-based questions. Language Direction Awareness (LDA) simply means we cultivate an understanding of how words pull our unconscious mind towards problems or solutions and how we can change what we say to influence the direction. LDA can be developed naturally by imagining a line labeled 'Problems' at one end and 'Solutions' at the other, and then noticing how your self-talk is moving you closer to either end. Statements have a neutral effect and make little difference to your position on the line, but the right kind of question will take you from one end to the other instantly.

Exercise

Whenever you feel trapped by thoughts of low self-esteem, worry or anxiety, ask yourself one or both of these questions:

1. Where would I rather be now?
2. How would I like to feel now ?

When you catch yourself saying 'I can't ...', ask yourself one or both of these questions:

1. Who says?
2. What would it be like if I could?

In order to find an answer, our unconscious mind must explore solutions rather than problems, and in doing so, it creates internal images of a desired outcome. This establishes an automatic flow towards positive thinking, and determines whether we spend our lives thinking about what we don't want and why we are unhappy, or developing the solutions required for lasting positive change.

In the beginning was the Word.
John 1:1

We can all improve our lives and be happier if we simply raise our awareness of the power of our words. If we criticize ourselves and others, we empower a self-destructive energy that affects every aspect of our lives. A mind that continuously criticizes actually weakens the immune system. Since everything we say resonates through our entire being, and because self-esteem is created by nourishing and valuing ourselves, we should cultivate a language based on kindness and love, both towards ourselves and others. This creates a nourishing energy that is reflected back into our lives in many ways. When we invite our unconscious mind to look for the good in others, it learns to filter automatically for that kind of information, not only in relation to other people but also to our own self-image. We may decide that the mindless habit of criticizing others is one habit we can't afford to keep.

Impeccability of your word can lead you to personal freedom, to huge success and abundance; it will take away all fear and transform it into joy and love.
Don Miguel Ruiz, author of *The Four Agreements*

What does 'impeccability of your word' mean and how can we practice it?

'Impeccable' means faultless or perfect, so impeccability of your word means keeping your words free from fault-finding and criticism. When you commit to this non-judgmental habit of speaking, a major shift takes place almost at once: you start to feel a new dynamic energy in your life and you begin to see things differently, perhaps most notably yourself. What a powerful and easy way to increase your self-esteem and general happiness! Just for today, refuse to make any verbal criticism or judgments about anyone. If others are gossiping or criticizing someone, stay out of it, and if you have to speak, make sure you say something positive.

Just for one day – how hard could that be?

If you wish, try it for half a day, or an hour or two; everyone can go an hour without criticizing someone. But the challenge is to go a whole day in which you keep your word impeccable, after which you'll be eligible for a very useful and interesting experiment. At some point in the evening, perhaps just before you go to bed, sit quietly and center yourself; empty your mind and relax for a few moments, breathing gently.

Now invite your mind to be aware of any changes in your energy.

If your words have been kind and nurturing throughout the whole day, you will now notice a change; it may be very slight or surprisingly strong, but it will be clearly noticeable when you are relaxed. What you are experiencing is simply the energy of your true self emerging. It's a part of you that isn't interested in any of the fear-based illusions of the ego and holds the power to transform them into joy and love. When you consider these changes to yourself after just one day, imagine what could change if you remain impeccable with your words for a week or a month. Your unconscious mind will be trained to search for the positive angle in every situation, and the compound interest generated by this change of direction will filter into in every aspect of your life.

A man cannot be comfortable without his own approval.
Mark Twain

We've been talking to ourselves about ourselves for quite a long time now, though not always with the same respect we show to others. If we spoke to our friends in the way we speak to ourselves, we probably wouldn't have any friends! Fortunately, we'd never dream of doing so. Sometimes our internal dialogue becomes so toxic and destructive we wish we could take a break away from ourselves, but wherever we go, that familiar voice shows up too, converting every mistake into a stick with which to beat ourselves. We know we weren't born with this self-deprecating commentary, and since we must have switched it on at some point we can also switch it off. One of the most effective ways to interrupt this program is, once again, to ask questions. Solution-focused questions make it harder to run the habits of self-deprecation and we can further support this by posing questions about what we feel grateful for in our lives. This may sound obvious, but research shows that anxiety, stress and depression create a state of mind in which it becomes difficult to see the positive resources all around us.

Consider the abundance that flows into your daily life. Cultivating gratitude nourishes our state of mind, moving us effortlessly beyond the repressive grip of the ego and its illusion of unworthiness. Recently I received an e-mail that reminds us of the good fortune we share in being who we are and where we are. It also provides another reminder of how quickly we can change our emotional state by seeing things from a different perspective. In fact the message invites us to see the whole world in an entirely different way, challenging our beliefs about those who share this planet with us. I have no idea who sent this e-mail to me, but it's enough to have received it. I am grateful for its stark reminder of so much that I already knew but had somehow avoided thinking about.

I offer it here in the same format it came to me.

If we could shrink our entire world down to the size of a small village of just 100 people and if all the human ratios remained just as they are right now, this is what that global village would look like:

Of the 100 people in the village, 48 would be men and 52 would be women.

31 would be white and 69 would be non-white.

8 would be African, 21 would be European and 57 would be Asians.

6 of those 100 people would own 60% of the entire wealth in the village.

50 of them would suffer from malnutrition.

70 would be illiterate and 80 of the 100 villagers would live in poverty.

1 would be close to death and 1 would be close to birth.

Only 1 would own a computer, or have had a college education.

Therefore, if you bought this book for yourself, if you have education enough to read it, if you have food in your fridge (or even have a fridge) and somewhere to sleep each night, then you are richer than 75% of the people in this world. Furthermore, if you've never starved or been wrongfully imprisoned for your views, you are luckier than the 500 million other souls who have. If you have a reasonably good level of health then you're far more fortunate than the one million who will not live to be with us this time next week because of ill health. The presence of any small change in your pocket right now places you in the top 8% of the world's wealthiest people, because 92% of the people who share the planet with you have no money at all.

Questions that cultivate a sense of personal gratitude provide one of the most effective interruptions to established negative thinking patterns. In the illusion of negativity and unworthiness our attention turns inward and explores the very emotions that keep us stuck. By asking abundance questions, we shift it from inside to outside.

Human salvation lies in the hands of the creatively maladjusted.
Martin Luther King Jr

We live in a golden age of human development and the choices we make collectively now will impact the future well-being of our planet, while our individual choices will determine the future quality of our lives. We should choose wisely now, mindful that the power to influence our future happiness lies within us, determined by the thoughts we allow to occupy our mind. The voice in your head isn't about to take a vow of silence, so you may as well be listening to a supportive friend rather than a destructive critic. Trying to close down your internal lines of communication hasn't worked up to now, so why not try the opposite approach? Start asking yourself the kind of questions that direct your unconscious mind towards solutions and make it hard for your critical internal voice to get started.

If you were having a conversation with someone and there was a topic you wanted to avoid, what would you do? Would you ask questions that were closely related to it, or questions that gently guide the conversation in an unrelated direction? Although words may be little more than an audio label we attach to experiences, LDA teaches us to be aware that they critically impact who we believe we are. Your challenge now is simply to raise your awareness of how you speak to yourself and others, and to cultivate a habit of asking questions that direct your attention towards where you'd like to be and what you feel grateful for.

Quick Start: Resources

Ten redirection questions

1. What has been the most useful part of this book so far?
2. Why was this particularly useful?
3. When have I felt more confident during the last week?
4. Where was I when I felt that increase in confidence?
5. Who else was there?
6. What made it easier for me to feel confident?
7. What else?
8. What single thing am I prepared to do differently each day?
9. What would I be prepared to stop doing?
10. What do I find easy to do that makes me feel more confident?

You may find it helpful to write down and keep your answers.

8

Fears, Failures and Comfort Zones

Awareness in itself is healing.
Fritz Perls

This chapter consists of three component parts in which we will explore the three factors which most commonly keep us stuck. The restoration of unconscious self-esteem must be an inside job, yet ironically it is there, in the realms of our mind, where we discover our most formidable dragons. The path to unconscious change will be easier once we learn to recognize and disempower the three fire-breathers most likely to stand in our way.

1. Fear

Fear is the main source of superstition and one of the main sources of cruelty. To conquer fear is the beginning of wisdom.
Bertrand Russell

It's been said that fear has the largest eyes. It certainly has the potential to be a destructive emotion, yet not all fear is bad. A little fear is necessary for our continued health and well-being. Toxic fears, the irrational haunting fears that keep us small, are the most debilitating of emotions, yet the kind of fear that prevents us from engaging in extremely risky or life-threatening activities provides a natural safety mechanism in our lives. Some years ago, while facilitating at a Life Balance course, I listened to a woman explaining how her life would be perfect if she could only remove all her fears. This might seem attractive to someone whose life is restricted by irrational fears but a life completely free of fear would probably be extremely exciting but also very short! For my part, if I had no fear at all, I'd drive a car through thick fog at 100 mph just for the buzz, I'd ski off the side of mountains, swim with great white sharks, and throw parachutes out of planes then dive out after them hoping I'd catch them on the way down. With no fear at all, I'd be lucky to live three months.

Fear has the potential to be our best friend or worst enemy. It's fine to have a little fear; it's not fine to let it pick you up and swing you round like a rag doll. To break free from the iron grip of irrational fear we must first acknowledge it, then change the way we see it. We can learn to recognize the subtle difference between toxic and rational fear and stop seeing it as a negative energy to be resisted, for in resisting rational fear we resist an essential aspect of our self.

All fear comes from within, which means a part of us is concerned enough about our well-being to generate an emotion that ensures a state of high alert. Instead of being angry and frustrated by this, we could choose to be grateful to the part of our being that cares enough about us to initiate the emotions of self-preservation.

We can view our fear as a part of our mind that wants to torment us or as a kindness born from a natural desire to stay safe. Fear is not the self-inflicted attack on your system that many believe it to be; in truth, what creature would be so unwise as to attack itself?

I've grown certain that the root of all fear is that we've been forced to deny who we are.
Frances Moore Lappé, O Magazine, May 2004

Acknowledging our natural desire to remain safe is the first step in overcoming the unhealthy effects of toxic fear, because it helps us realize that fear in essence is not a destructive energy; it is only our mindless misuse of it that makes it so. Much like fire, fear is useful but must also be watched closely and not overfed. A small fire serves us well, keeping us warm, lighting our darkness, and providing a way to cook our food. Yet the secret to its use lies in good management; if we feed it too much fuel it will quickly escalate out of our control and we may end up trying to fight what was once a useful resource. Our toxic fears are like a fire that has had too much fuel and not enough of our attention. When we allow this to happen, our ego mind fans the flames of our natural fight/flight response until it grows out of control. Again, no one is born with toxic irrational fears already in place; their cultivation is a learned pattern which we mindlessly allow to become established in our unconscious mind, and once established it will run an automatic search for something to worry about even when everything is going well.

This useless unconscious program can dominate every aspect of our lives. We worry that we aren't rich enough, pretty enough, slim enough, or that we don't measure up to other people's expectations – all worries born from toxic fears that diminish the quality of our lives. Yet these concerns are not really due to a lack of something in our lives; they're the result of habitual toxic conditioning. Once we allow fear to paralyze our mind, even the lowest level of self-esteem will seem beyond us. The way to break out of our toxic fear habits is to understand that they need 'fuel' in order to continue; without our input the toxic fears will die. The key to change, therefore, lies in learning how to stop feeding the fire.

Fear is the path to the dark side, fear leads to anger, anger leads to hate, hate leads to suffering.
Yoda (*Star Wars Episode 1*)

Story

An old Native American story tells of a young boy who at the fragile age between childhood and adulthood is finding the transition difficult. He feels an emerging desire to go and explore the world, to soar like an eagle in the exciting and sometimes dangerous world of adults. But another part of his young mind yearns to remain a child, safe in the familiar surroundings of his village. These two conflicting emotions are like an internal civil war raging within him, keeping him stuck. At last, unable to bear the frustration any longer, he seeks out the wisdom of his grandfather.

The boy explains that it feels like there are two wolves inside him, each fighting for control; one wolf is trying to keep him in the safety of the village while the other wolf wants him to spread his wings and live life to the full.

The old man listens quietly to his grandson's story, then says, 'What you are experiencing is fear of change and since change can sometimes be a little scary it's perfectly acceptable to experience a little fear. We all have two such wolves who show up and fight with each other whenever we face the challenges of change.'

The boy looks deep into the eyes of his grandfather and asks a new question.

'Tell me, Grandfather. Which wolf wins?'

The old man smiles. 'The one that I feed.'

* * *

We can learn much from our fears; we can learn that a part of us is trying to keep us safe, and also become mindful of how we set up and feed the unconscious fear patterns that keep us stuck. The wolves of fear will work for or against us, and we must be careful which one we feed, because the wrong wolf may make us its next meal.

The wise man in the storm prays to God, not for safety from danger, but deliverance from fear. It is the storm within which endangers him, not the storm without.
Ralph W. Emerson

2. Failure

It doesn't matter how many times you fall.
It only matters how many times you get up.
Japanese proverb

Almost every fear we have manifests itself as a visual fantasy in our mind. The word 'fear' can represent *F*antasized *E*xperiences *A*ppearing *R*eal. Not least among our many fears is the fantasy that we may fail to achieve a specific goal; in some cases the fear of failure will stop us before we even get started, primarily due to painful past associations we have unconsciously linked to the word. Rejection is often unconsciously perceived as failure, which may account for the high number of people who are reluctant to ask for what they want. This one word, 'failure', and the unconscious associations we have with it is the main reason that people give up on their goals and the primary reason why we feel so disinclined to ask for help – or even a date. We believe it will be emotionally safer not to ask. In reality, asking for help, for a date, or for anything else we may need can never leave us worse off than before we asked, since we presumably did not have what we were asking for to begin with. If we ask someone to help us in some way and they decline, we remain exactly as we were before we asked; in fact we could claim to be better off since we now know who doesn't want to help.

Can this small word really have such a limiting effect on our lives? After all, 'failure' is just a label used to describe our experiences and in objective reality experiences have no real meaning; they simply are.

Take as an example the experience we commonly label 'bad weather'.

When it rains heavily, we may call the experience 'bad' weather, yet the accuracy of this label depends on who is viewing the experience. The rain isn't bad for a farmer who has a valuable crop planted and has been worried about a lengthy spell of dry weather, though it would probably be bad to the organizers of a summer barbecue. In truth, the weather is neither good or bad without an observer who can give meaning to it, and the meaning we give to any experience is primarily influenced by the way we look at it. The different ways in which we can view the experiences in our life is called a 'frame' by the practitioners of NLP, a term which has its origins in the successful work of two therapists, Virginia Satir and Milton H. Erickson.

Frames can change, enhance, or diminish the meaning of any event, much like the cut-out cartoon images we find at a fair; we pop our face into the cut-out hole and instantly we resemble a cartoon character to anyone looking from the front. Frames make everything look different; some frames improve the look of things while others make them look worse. Our mind is pre-programmed to make sense of the world and search for meaning in every event, yet in our haste to label the experiences of our life we may also limit our ability to improve or alter them due to an unwise yet unconscious choice of frame.

There is nothing either good or bad, but thinking makes it so.
William Shakespeare

Story

A farmer once owned a thoroughbred stallion worth a great deal of money. One day, after feeding the horse, the farmer's son accidentally left the stable door ajar; the horse pushed it open and found himself untethered in the open farmyard. Faced with this rare freedom, he took one look out across the open fields and galloped off into the distance, leaving the farmer and son staring after him.

A neighbor standing nearby turned to the farmer and said, 'That was bad luck.'

To which the farmer simply replied, 'Perhaps.'

A few days later, to their great surprise, the stallion returned, followed closely by two wild mares. The farmer and his son quickly caught all three horses and secured them in a nearby paddock. The same neighbor witnessed this apparent stroke of good fortune and ruefully remarked, 'That was good luck.'

Again the farmer replied 'Perhaps.'

Sometime later the son began to break in one of the wild mares, was thrown off, and suffered a broken leg from the fall. The neighbor offered his condolences: 'That was bad luck.'

Once more, the farmer simply shrugged his shoulders and said 'Perhaps.'

The following week, the army arrived in the local village to recruit young men to fight in a war, but the farmer's son was excused from service due to his injuries.

The neighbor once more offered his view of the situation. 'That was good luck,' he said.

You've probably guessed by now what the farmer said in reply.

* * *

Only hindsight can reveal whether an event will turn out to be good or bad. It may seem difficult to feel upbeat after a job interview that ended with rejection, yet we can change our emotional response to that rejection by altering the frame in which we view it. Time may show that rejection in a different light; hindsight may reveal it to be the best thing that could possibly have happened to us, because we later landed a better job we wouldn't have applied for had the first interview been successful. Many of our so-called problem events seem worse as a result of the frame we put them in; yet by changing the frame of any event we can change its meaning, and when we change what it means to us, we automatically change how we unconsciously respond to it.

Failure versus feedback

The labels we mindlessly attach to events can stop our progress in a second. Viewing an event as a 'failure' may have devastating effects on our resolve to continue, primarily due to unconscious negative associations we have with the word. Anyone who frames unsuccessful experiences in this way will be less inclined to embrace new challenges since the painful emotions they associate with the possibility of failure will damage what may already be a fragile self-image.

The negative emotional associations of failure may have begun a long time ago when we were young children. Perhaps we were told at school that those who don't work hard enough become failures, or perhaps we learned to associate a grade F with *failure*. Later, while still at an impressionable age, we may have heard someone who is unsuccessful in life described as 'a failure'. Amidst all this unconscious conditioning, it is easy to establish painful unconscious associations to every subsequent lack of success.

So damaging are the effects of this unconscious association that NLP practitioners use an expression that changes the frame in which they regard unsuccessful outcomes, for by changing the frame of the outcome, they also change the impact it has on their unconscious mind: *There's no such thing as failure, only feedback.*

This is an extremely useful statement for our unconscious mind to hear. It suggests that we can only learn more about something and never less, that every new attempt to do something moves us inevitably closer to it by providing valuable information we did not already have, in the form of feedback. Feedback is simply information that arrives in two forms which we are taught to label 'positive' or 'negative', yet in truth both are equally useful since we can learn as much from what doesn't work as we can from what does.

There's a story about Thomas Edison which illustrates this

point. Edison, in his attempts to invent the light filament, applied electricity through many different mediums until after some 200 unsuccessful attempts he finally succeeded. At the following press briefing, a young reporter congratulated Edison for his determination, especially in the face of so many prior *failures*. Edison shook his head in disagreement and calmly replied, 'Sir, I didn't have any failures; I simply discovered 200 things that didn't work.'

If we think about Edison's response, he was simply reframing every unsuccessful attempt by perceiving it as *feedback* from which he could learn something. By doing this, he was able to continue his work until he eventually found the solution. This means we can't really be regarded as a failure at anything as long as we produce information we can learn from, and by learning what does and doesn't work, like Edison, we'll eventually discover what we're looking for.

If we try unsuccessfully to achieve a goal and tell ourselves we 'failed', our willpower to try again will drain away. If we do manage to muster enough energy to try a second time, we may do so with our self-belief severely depleted. However, if we reframe our first attempt by reframing how we view what happened, our self-belief will remain strong. By changing the word 'failure' to 'feedback' we change our response because the word 'feedback' is highly unlikely to have any previously established unconscious negative associations for us. Failure is an expensive frame in which to place our experiences of the world, and the price we ultimately pay for doing so may rob us of our dreams. In truth, the only way we can really fail is by choosing to give up on our goal and to quit, and thankfully in most cases that choice is entirely ours to make.

You never really lose until you quit trying.
Mike Ditka

The challenge now is to remove the word 'failure' from your vocabulary for a total of 30 days, replacing it with the word 'feedback'. All you need do is reframe any unsuccessful outcome by seeing it as a form of feedback. During this 30-day period, you should not only try to stop using the word 'failure' in relation to your own unsuccessful outcomes but also in relation to anyone else. Now when you return to a goal you once gave up on, you won't regard your earlier unsuccessful attempt as a failure; you'll see it as feedback – which is only information. It's there to be useful to you; it's the universe's way of letting you know what works well and what doesn't so you can adjust your strategy and do something different.

Whatever we try to achieve in life will produce feedback in some form. It rarely comes with a positive or negative label already attached, yet we inevitably attach labels to everything, in order to make sense of our world. This is a natural compulsion, yet we should give some thought to which labels empower our resolve to try again and which keep us trapped in the self-restricting trance of failure, which labels increase our unconscious sense of self-esteem and which quickly diminish it.

Reframing failure into feedback is a habit that is easily developed. Once your mind gets used to seeing things differently, any unsuccessful outcomes you experience will have no power to weaken your resolve to try again because you feel you are continuously learning something new and useful. Most people feel unhappy when they think they failed, yet almost everyone is happy to learn something new.

Our unconscious mind will elicit more positive information from an experience than our conscious attempt to do so. In fact, sometimes in our enthusiasm to learn more, we may be inclined to overanalyze or misinterpret what took place. Once again, our ability to ask the right questions about an unsuccessful experience empowers our unconscious mind to learn. Try asking these three specific questions:

1. What can I learn from this experience?
2. What are the positives in it?
3. What could I do differently as a result of what I now know?

These solution-focused questions generate an unconscious search for ways to improve the situation and move you closer to your goals. We should learn to regard positive and negative feedback alike; after all, since they're equally valuable, they are both welcome.

Failure is a signpost on the road to success that says you're going the wrong way.
Jack Canfield, co-author of *A Little Chicken Soup for the Soul*

As we journey along life's pathway, we'll be fortunate to always be successful in our first attempt to do anything new. Since most of us will create at least as many unsuccessful outcomes as successful ones, we should frame our experiences in a way that strengthens rather than weakens our determination to continue.

Don't allow your past disappointments to determine your future success; everyone who succeeds was unsuccessful to begin with. Walt Disney was allegedly fired from his first job for having 'no imagination'! Abraham Lincoln had the modern equivalent of three months' schooling, was unsuccessful in business at the age of 21 and again at 24, lost the same electoral race on two separate occasions, and had a nervous breakdown at the age of 27. Edgar Allen Poe was expelled from school and Thomas Edison had to leave school for continuously being bottom of his class. Benjamin Franklin was regarded by teachers as being 'very poor at maths' and inventor James Watt was labeled 'dull' and 'inept'. It doesn't really matter what others think of our efforts since their opinion is no more than a reflection of their perception of their world. As a teenager, John Lennon was often told by his aunt, 'Music's all right, John, but you'll never make any money out of it.'

Our ability to keep going when we most feel like quitting influences the results we achieve, and the way we label the events in our life determines when or even if we quit. The negative emotions we can associate to the word 'failure' could keep us small and stop us ever realizing our dreams.

We've seen two of the three 'dragons' that can stand between us and the changes we seek, yet there's a third, equally powerful, that we will almost certainly find blocking our way. This one not only affects each new challenge we face, but directly influences what we choose as a goal, who we think we should be with, and our unconscious level of self-esteem.

3. Comfort Zones

Everything you've ever wanted lies just outside your comfort zone.
Robert Allen, co-author of *The One-Minute Millionaire*

A comfort zone is a learned state of psychological or physical comfort in which we feel no sense of risk or anxiety and we may feel naturally drawn by its compelling illusion of safety.

In a typical comfort zone we remain where we feel safe, never stretching our mind or testing our resolve against the challenges of life; instead we play safe, treating challenge and risk as the domain of children and fools. People who are trapped in the grip of a comfort zone quickly become uncomfortable when faced with new challenges.

Yet the reality is that we are by nature creatures of growth. Our mind is designed to develop and stretch with every new challenge; when we set goals that seem to be beyond our current abilities, something within us unconsciously searches for a way to achieve them.

A comfort zone has its foundations set in fear – fear of change, fear that we may not measure up in some way, or fear that something bad may happen if we stop doing what we've always done. Comfort zones can keep people trapped in toxic relationships for years through the fear that they will be unable to cope alone. Change involves a degree of risk, which the comfort zone associates with fear, and in an attempt to avoid the fearful images that accompany the risk we allow our comfort zone to keep us safe where we are. But this security comes at a price. By remaining where we are, we stay stuck in what may be a very damaging and toxic situation.

Comfort zones also influence our unconscious sense of self-esteem by fear. Staying inactive enforces the limitations of the comfort zone boundaries and we may find ourselves locked in the grip of a self-perpetuating cycle of confinement.

In certain parts of India, people train a baby elephant by tethering one of its legs to a stake in the ground; the animal can move around within an area determined by the length of the rope. The baby elephant may try occasionally to break the tether but soon learns that the rope is too strong, for a baby. After a time, it stops trying to break the rope and accepts the situation. Years later, when the baby has matured into a full-grown adult, it continues to be confined by the same rope even though it now has more than enough strength to snap it with ease. The elephant therefore is no longer confined by the rope but by an experience it learned when young. A comfort zone is similar to the rope that holds the elephant; both may keep us safe but they will also keep us stuck and restrict every effort we make to break free. Indeed, both the rope that holds the elephant and our comfort zone are much easier to break than they seem.

Comfort zones are extremely restrictive to our development but they are also extremely flexible and will quickly realign in accordance with each new learning or challenge. Take learning to drive a car, for example. The first time someone gets behind the wheel of a car they experience a huge shift in their comfort zone; they have to coordinate hand and feet movements in synchronization with clutch and gear activity. It's not easy and takes most beginners beyond the edges of their comfort zone. Some people will find themselves so far out of their comfort zone after their first driving lesson that they even want to quit. Fortunately, this desire to quit diminishes as their skills improve and they discover that what was uncomfortable to begin with is now becoming less so, as their comfort zone expands and realigns with their new learning. No matter how uncomfortable we might feel when we step beyond the boundaries of our comfort zone, that discomfort quickly diminishes if we stay on the edge of our boundaries.

If you are hopeful, of course you can take action. The miracle occurs when you don't feel much hope, yet you push yourself into action anyway. Perhaps it's the brain, stimulated by the action, that brings you back to hope. I don't know why it works, I just know it does.
Shari Lewis

The comfort zone sustains itself and draws strength from routine; therefore, an effective way to step beyond its hold lies in doing things differently. The more difference you bring to your life, the weaker your comfort zone will become, primarily because your comfort zone is influenced by your unconscious mind and your unconscious mind loves routine.

For some reason, when things start to go badly in our life we seem to become even less flexible than usual; we stick to the same routine, repeating the same unsuccessful strategies over and over. But as the old saying reminds us, if you always do what you've always done, you'll always get what you've always had. The trick to breaking free from a comfort zone lies in creating as much difference in your life as possible, since differences provide the unconscious mind with new information, and anything new or different will disrupt the patterns of routine that support the comfort zone.

So what can we do differently?

Well, anything, especially things that may seem like a stretch to you. If you set yourself a goal that you believe is *just beyond* your present ability, you will discover that in nine out of every ten cases you will achieve your goal. This is because we're all more capable than we may currently believe, and only when we stretch ourselves in pursuit of a particular goal do we make this discovery. When people go 'all out' to make a business deadline, they succeed in most instances; they somehow find a way to do whatever it takes – and probably surprise themselves in the process.

What about lifestyle routines? They provide the greatest source of potential change. For example, if you always meet a particular friend on Wednesday mornings at a specific place, do something different: go on Wednesday afternoon instead, or on Monday. You could also change the location, or you could even invite a different person to come along. Our unconscious mind loves routine and such changes, however small, create quite a positive stir in the subliminal pool. Just be careful to only introduce changes that are totally safe and healthy to your well-being.

Clothes are another unconscious source of routine. It's thought the average man wears 20% of his entire clothing collection 80% of the time. Women are typically much more flexible, though they also tend to be conditioned by a degree of sameness. Some women say they never wear a particular color, perhaps because they believe it doesn't suit them. But this belief presents an excellent opportunity to push the buttons of change by introducing something different and stretching your comfort zone at the same time. Commit to wearing that prohibited color for just a day or even half a day and notice what happens when you relax with it. Who knows? You may even receive compliments on your appearance and decide you have been wrong about that color.

Take a new (and safe) route to work, to school, to anywhere you regularly visit; go at a different time, a little earlier or later than usual, depending on your commitments. Start thinking about hobbies you have always thought might be interesting but never got around to starting. Consider taking a course in a subject that would stretch your comfort zone; learn a language, read a book you would not normally choose, listen to a genre of music you previously regarded as 'not really my thing'. In short, think of as many ways you can introduce newness or a change of direction to everything you do. You'll be pleasantly surprised at how many things you can change, primarily because we tend to establish fixed habits of routine in which we drift mindlessly through life in the same old way, producing the same old results.

We are the most flexible and creative thinkers on this planet; every other life form is a specialist in their field but none can demonstrate the flexibility of the human mind. A frog is an expert fly catcher, designed to notice small black insects that pass within reach of its tongue. Anyone who has ever seen a slow-motion film of its elongated tongue unfurling at high speeds to catch even the fastest fly in mid-flight will appreciate its amazing skill. Yet for all this skill, the frog possesses little by way of flexibility, for it will starve to death if left in a box of dead flies. You and I, however, have a gift unique to our species: we can think flexibly and creatively, review our routine behaviors, and consider where we could introduce change, for even the slightest change in routine can create a world of difference.

We are all influenced by our comfort zone at a level unique to each of us; some are confined by it and remain stuck in the illusion of safety, while others make a commitment to lifelong learning and see challenges as opportunities. Only you can evaluate if your comfort zone is serving you or if it keeps you confined in the illusion of safety from something you need not fear at all: your personal growth. If you decide you've allowed your comfort zone to hold you back, simply remember the baby elephant and what keeps it stuck. A comfort zone is a learned state. It has no power to confine you anymore than the rope can confine the elephant, and the way to break free lies in realizing our true power to change things. Learn to be comfortable with the initial temporary discomfort of new challenges and small differences to your routine. The excitement generated by each new step we take positively impacts our unconscious self-image and inspires us to stretch and grow further. If you'd like to feel that sense of excitement and create something different in the future, you must first do something different today.

> *When you discover you are riding a dead horse, the best strategy is to dismount.*
> Dakota tribal proverb

We now know the three dragons most likely to bar our way. In identifying them we are better equipped to overcome each as we meet them, though unlike the fabled knights of old, we won't need to travel far to locate our dragons. They reside within and may appear as soon as we take our first steps on the journey of change. Understanding how these factors may restrict our progress is an essential aspect of unconscious re-programming, though we should also be mindful that their power to stop us increases if we are tired, or uncertain of the way forward. Unconscious self-esteem flows effortlessly when we feel rested and comfortable with who we are and the underlying purpose of our life, yet to make such discoveries we must look beneath the surface illusion of our conscious mind. Psychiatry has largely taught us to fear the realm of the unconscious mind, but in truth we have nothing to fear but fear itself, for here in the realm of the unconscious we gain our first glimpse of our true self and the real purpose of our lives.

The path to unconscious confidence and self-esteem lies in greater awareness of self and purpose. As we grow older, it becomes easier to lose sight of our true nature. We're so easily seduced by the self-fulfilling illusions of intolerance and fear. Our awareness shrinks when it should be expanding, and we mindlessly allow unconscious conditioning to attract unhealthy damaging emotions rather than the wisdom and love which is our true essence.

Authentic awareness of self comes not from any cognitive analysis of behavior, of mood or the good opinion of others, but from the experience of self. Fortunately, we can return our attention to this fundamental presence very easily – through the ancient practice of meditation.

The practice of meditation powerfully contributes to our rich collection of resources but also provides something else, something that is far more useful in creating unconscious self-esteem than anything we have so far learned. It provides an invaluable reminder of who we really are.

Quick Start: Resources
Doing something different
Where could you stretch yourself in some small way today?

Set one goal today that will stretch your comfort zone just slightly.

Change just one small thing in your routine today.

Choose one or more of the following suggestions and commit to it for just one day.

1. Wear a different style, color, or type of clothing.
2. Take a different (safe) route to your destination.
3. Change your hairstyle.
4. Alter a regular part of your routine in one small way.
5. Read something you would never usually read.
6. Listen to a genre of music that you rarely listen to.
7. Eat at a slightly different time.
8. Volunteer to help someone in need.

9. Find one new way to laugh more.
10. Give away an item of clothing you haven't worn in the last five years.

Any change to your routine, no matter how small, will have an unconscious effect.

The above list is merely a short selection of small changes; your ideas will be as good if not better than these.

Take some time to be creative and think of as many small and *safe* ways to bring as much difference to your daily routine as possible. Remember, little fish are very sweet!

9

Catching the Waves

Self-realization means that we have been consciously connected with our source of being, and once we have made this connection, nothing can go wrong.
Swami Paramananda

High self-esteem automatically generates high self-confidence and requires no conscious effort to maintain, whereas any conscious attempt to feel better about ourselves requires a lot of effort and is usually quite ineffective. Anyone who has tried to like themselves more can confirm this. The path to unconscious self-esteem lies not in any conscious efforts to feel happier but in the principle of least effort. In fact any unconscious change must by definition require no conscious effort at all. The secret to greater happiness lies in re-programming our unconsciously held perception of self, and this transformation begins effortlessly the moment we recognize our true self and realize that we are much more than the 'I' with which we commonly identify ourselves.

This overused singular pronoun unconsciously associates who we think we are with a name or label – our life story, our possessions, our emotions and behaviors. But we can never actually *be* the temporary transient events and labels in our life; we can only experience them as they arise and fade in our awareness.

If you relax your mind and completely switch off from the constant buzz and clamor of life, your attention automatically turns inward and you may become aware of another part of you which exists beyond the labels of 'I' and 'me'. This subtle awareness provides a brief glimpse of who you really are beyond the illusions of the ego mind. Perhaps you've been vaguely aware of this underlying background presence most of your life or perhaps you've never given it a thought until now; either way, it has always been there, silently observing the passing universe from the center of your being.

This presence isn't your mind. It's the observer of your mind; it's your higher self. This is the part of you that knows exactly what you need to help and sustain you at every step of this journey you have chosen, and because it's a part of you it's available wherever you are at any time. Put this book down now for a moment and relax, then place your attention inside your body and notice how it feels from inside. Notice any slight tingle or sensations occurring as you move your attention from inside one part to another, from your hands up to your shoulders, into your abdomen and down to your feet. Now as you experience this, try to get a sense of where *you* are located in this body of yours. Where can you be found? Is it in your mind, your heart, your eyes – or are you located in every place at the same time? You may become intuitively aware of a subtle energy that can't be defined as your physical body or mind, or even the voice in your mind, which many mistakenly believe to represent who they are.

If it were possible to be the voice in your mind then who is it speaking to? You are not your mind or its ego-driven voice; you are a silent observer of your conscious mind and all it thinks and says. Without an observer, surely your thoughts would simply stream out in a constant flow as does the visual content of your dreams. Our greatest resource in transforming our sense of self lies in understanding that we are not what we see in the mirror; we are that which observes what we see there. In raising your awareness of this simple truth you initiate a sense of awakening; a subtle shift occurs as your unconscious mind begins to realign with your true sense of self – an infinite source of unconscious self-esteem and abundance in every area of your life.

Where there is peace and meditation there is neither anxiety or doubt.
St Francis of Assisi

Far too many people never think of looking for happiness within but have embarked on a mission to acquire the external things we believe we need in order to be happy. This belief is an illusion created by our ego mind when, in reality, nothing could be further from the truth. We have created a culture that seduces young minds into believing that happiness is created externally, that if we have enough money we must be happier. Of course, if that were true there would be no such thing as a depressed millionaire and no one could feel happy while living in the slums of Mumbai.

The moment we adopt this illusion of external reference, we initiate a state of mind which is constantly driven by the belief that it needs to get something in order to feel complete. We become like the cartoon image of the donkey chasing a carrot dangling from a stick just ahead of him; no matter how fast he runs, he can never get the carrot. So it is with the mind that seeks self-worth externally: no matter how much praise we receive, no matter what we buy, an uneasy sense of discontentment remains. The chattering voice of the ego mind tells us we can only be happy if we meet Mr Right or Miss Perfect, when we get that perfect job, the promotion or the new car. Even if we won millions on the national lottery and bought all the things we believed would make us happy, we would always have an underlying sense that something essential was missing in our lives. We might feel different in the short term, but eventually we'd realize we feel no different than we did to begin with.

The truth is that everyone already has all the resources they will ever need to create greater happiness and abundance in every area of their lives. The most materially referenced people in the world actually know this is true. They are unlikely to know it consciously but they know it experientially; they sense, as do we, that designer labels, fast cars or whatever else the ego identifies with are not essential for greater happiness. They might be nice, but they're not essential ingredients in the recipe.

Your true nature is one of internal reference. You draw your sense of self-worth from within. At source, there is a part of you with a very different agenda to that of your ego-driven mind. This is your true self, the real 'you', the 'you' that is not interested which designer label you wear or which car you drive. Your true self has no interest in the endless shopping list of the ego mind and wants just one thing: to be at peace and enjoy the journey you have chosen. This is the fundamental aspect of your being that wants you to live your life to the outer edges of your skin; to be all that you can be, running toward life's challenges, not away from them; to embrace each new experience on the path that lies ahead with optimism and excitement. Conversely, the illusions of the ego mind teach us to measure self-worth through the filters of comparison, criticizing or blaming ourselves if we don't compare favorably with others. We don't have to measure our self-worth in this way. We can learn to *know it* instinctively through a clearer understanding of our true essence.

Self-awareness is the key to high self-esteem and greater happiness in every area of our lives, for in that moment of self-realization everything changes. Yet this transformational realization is not founded on beliefs about ourselves, because what we believe may prove to be false. It is founded on intuitive certainty, an all-pervading awareness of self which transcends beliefs and the fears of the ego-driven mind. It is there, in our most natural and original state of awareness, where we need no advice on which career to follow or who to share our life with. In this state, unconscious self-esteem flows effortlessly, for we are at one with ourselves and everything else in the universe, though we must understand that it cannot be realized in a mind that contains no self-worth or love for itself.

Transformation comes from looking deeply within, to a state that exists before fear and isolation arise, the state in which we are inviolably whole just as we are. We connect to ourselves, to our own true experience, and discover there, that to be alive means to be whole.

Sharon Salzberg

When an interviewer asked the Dalai Lama why so many people in the West seemed to suffer from low self-esteem, he looked at him with a puzzled expression on his face. The interpreter sitting next to him realized the term 'low self-esteem' had no meaning in Tibetan culture, so he rephrased the question in a way the Tibetan leader might more easily understand. This only seemed to increase the confusion, as did each new attempt the interpreter made to pose the question, until suddenly, with a look of amazement, the Dalai Lama asked in disbelief, 'But why would anyone do this to themselves?'

The most peaceful and effective way to access this natural state of awareness lies in the regular practice of meditation, for it is there, in the space between thoughts, that the ego-driven voice in our head finally falls silent. This is where we find the inner realm which Dr Wayne Dyer calls 'the gap'. 'The gap' refers to the subtle non-judgmental space between every thought, a timeless void of infinite nothingness in which we can simply *be*. This non-thinking oasis of peace and stillness is a rare state of expanded consciousness. In the main, we permit our attention to drift mindlessly from one thought to another, unaware of any space which exists between. Yet it is here in the space between thoughts that we find our true essence; this is where infinite possibilities and potentiality abound. Here we find peace and learn who we really are. We do not find ourselves contained in our thoughts anymore than we can be contained in our reflection, as the Zen saying reminds us: 'It is the space between the bars that holds the tiger.'

Our thoughts seem to flow continuously in and out of our awareness with seamless continuity, though in truth a small almost imperceptible space exists between each of them. Thinking usually follows a cycle of cause and effect: we think something, which then almost instantly triggers another related thought, which in turn triggers the next one, and so on. For the most part we allow this endless river of mindlessness to flow through our conscious awareness unchecked. By becoming mindfully aware, we can slow this flow down enough to notice the gaps between each passing thought, and if we stop it completely, even if only for a few moments, we will slip into the silent space between thoughts and enter 'the gap'. The practice of meditation is the fastest and most effective way to achieve this. Just a few minutes' practice each day trains your thinking to slow down and eventually stop, and eventually you will find you are able to slip into the gap with relative ease.

Unconscious self-esteem automatically begins the moment you awake to who you really are. Daily meditation practice dissolves the illusions of the ego mind and reawakens an authentic sense of self. This is one of the most valuable gifts we could give ourselves. The trance of unworthiness we call 'low self-esteem' requires an illusion in order to sustain itself. We must continue to believe *we are* our behavior, our name, our job title, or the role we play in family or society, yet as our practice of meditation develops, we begin to see that these identity illusions can never represent who we really are at source. By spending a few minutes each day in silent meditation we can create a strong sense of inner peace; we feel happier, more relaxed, and more aware of our true self.

It's no coincidence that every ancient spiritual teaching in the world acknowledges the use of meditation as a way to increase our sense of purpose and spirituality, yet in spite of this, meditation continues to remain something of a mystery to many in the West who see it as the weird practice of Tibetan monks or hippies. The reality, however, is that we don't need to live in a cave in the Himalayas for ten years to learn how to meditate; we can achieve a good level of skill without leaving our home. Meditation is not a form of religion and does not require its participants to give up anything; therefore, it can be safely practiced by followers of all faiths without fear of compromising personal beliefs. Meditation is simply a way to transcend the confines of the ego mind to find happiness in stillness and peace – what we really are at source. You won't need the advice of an expert or guru; in fact, as with all internal aspects of your being, *you* are the only adviser you will ever need.

What you will need to find is an opportunity in each day to be still and relaxed for two to three minutes. Once you become accustomed to doing this, you can gradually increase your meditation time by five minutes until you reach the point where you can comfortably sit for 20 minutes at a time in each day.

There's now a growing awareness in Western culture of the many benefits associated with daily meditation, thanks to an increasing amount of reliable research confirming the critical role it can play in healing and well-being. Researchers at Stanford University in California compared over 100 different methods of relaxation and found clear evidence that Transcendental Meditation was more than twice as effective as any other form of relaxation. Transcendental Meditation (TM) was introduced to the West in the late 1950s and early 1960s by Maharishi Mahesh Yogi who numbered The Beatles and Deepak Chopra among his students. Scientific study of those practicing TM shows that practitioners who meditate regularly will require 50% fewer hospital visits and experience on average 70% fewer cases of heart-related disease.

In 1993 a number of British doctors were so impressed with the findings of these and other studies that they petitioned the Secretary for Health to make TM available to all customers in the National Health Service (NHS). Since TM isn't very different from other meditation styles, we can assume that regular practice of meditation in any format will yield the same restorative and healing effects.

Interestingly, the word 'meditation' originates from the Latin word *mederi* which means 'to heal'. Indeed we can do much to heal and nourish our whole system simply by making meditation a regular routine for a few minutes each day. Knowing this, of course, is one thing; establishing it into a daily practice is quite another, primarily because our active conscious mind is not used to us asking it to be still for any length of time.

All man's miseries stem from his inability to sit silently in a room and do nothing.
Blaise Pascal, 17th century scientist

Our 21st century lives require skilled feats of balancing, as everybody seems to want a slice of our attention and our time. Sadly, in doing our best we may forget to slow down and do nothing. Many people relax physically but never think to provide a similar respite for their mind, yet it is here in the silent stillness of non-thought that relaxation is truly found. When did you last close your eyes and empty your mind of visual and auditory stimulation? Meditation is not sitting quietly, thinking positive thoughts; when we do this, the mind continues to be active, since positive thinking is just more thinking, and thinking will usually move our attention away from the present and on to past or future events. This means we aren't fully present in the current moments of our life. On the contrary, meditation is non-thinking, a state of mind in which we observe our thoughts rather than become involved with them. It offers a peaceful haven of rest for our mind and since we wouldn't dream of staying physical active 24/7 without rest, why should we expect it of our mind?

When they begin meditating, people often expect their mind to immediately switch off and stop what it's doing. We expect to be able to switch off the ceaseless flow of visual and audio stimulation, just as we might flick off a light switch. But the usual response from our undisciplined mind is a strong reluctance to enter into this new, unfamiliar game. Our thoughts have been like a never-ending waterfall all our lives and as soon as we try to take control of this flow, a new thought pops up almost immediately.

Our mind is programmed to think, and it's been doing so for a long time. Imagine allowing a small child to run around your home unchecked and out of control; then after some years, you suddenly ask it to be still and quiet. How would that child respond? Would your request be granted? Similarly, our mind has been allowed to run wild, and perhaps for the first time you are asking it to do something it has never been asked to do before.

Fortunately, it's never too late to teach our mind to react differently. In the simple act of breathing, we have a natural way to train our mind to be still and prepare it for the practice of meditation.

> *In everyday life we rarely pay full attention to anything whereas in meditation we commit ourselves exclusively to doing just that.*
>
> *When you pay full attention to anything (or to nothing), it becomes a spiritual practice.*
>
> Dan Millman, *Everyday Enlightenment*

Scientific tests show measurable physical improvements in people who meditate regularly, such as a lowering of blood pressure, reduced stress, healthier immune systems and higher levels of concentration. If this is not enough incentive, it also significantly improves our sense of self-worth!

So what exactly happens when we meditate?

We enter a state of heightened consciousness in which we become singularly focused in the present moment. Our chattering internal voice at last falls silent, allowing inner peace to pervade a world of non-judgmental thought – a state we refer to as 'mindfulness'. Mindfulness does not mean you're in a trance or in any way switched off from what is happening around you. In fact it's the opposite; you know exactly where you are and you are fully awake in the present moment, the 'now' – the only place you can ever really be. Mindfulness allows your attention to focus on 'what is' without the need to apply meaning or logic to it.

In the final moments of the Buddha's life, his followers gathered around and asked him, 'Who are you? Tell us – are you God, are you the son of God, are you the messiah?'

The Buddha smiled and said, 'I am none of those things. I am simply awake.'

Meditation is a way to be more awake. When you are 'awake', you know who you are, and the ego-driven problems of low self-esteem vanish along with every other fear-based internal conflict. This awareness of self can't be contained in words or explained by the labels of cognitive thought; it can only really be known experientially. Meditation enhances our perception of reality through expanded consciousness, transcending the illusions created by our ego mind. Low self-esteem can only exist in a mind seduced by the illusions of the ego, primarily because in that state of self-deception we are not fully aware of the negative unconscious programming that keeps us so firmly stuck.

Meditation provides a tool to remove our fear-based judgmental illusions and create greater happiness. Too often we experience the present moments of our lives as fragments of time, fractions of experience, focused on what we've done or will do next. Examples of this present-moment mindlessness are almost everywhere, perhaps most notably in the faces of friends who arrange to meet with each other, then sit there, each absorbed in reading and sending text messages to someone else. They thus miss the experience of being with the person they arranged to be with. Meditation is a way to mindfully focus our attention singularly into the present moment.

> *Within you rests the Universal answers to every question you could ever ask yourself.*
>
> *It's been said that prayer is talking to God ... meditation is listening.*
>
> *Can you hear the Universe whispering to you?*
> davidji

Unfortunately, a lot of nonsense is talked about meditation; people tell you they are 'into' meditation and describe how wonderful their life is because of the insight it brings. Most of them mean well, but experience has taught me that those who get the most benefit from meditation don't talk about it; they simply do it. Such talk can be counterproductive by creating doubts in the minds of beginners about whether they're doing it right and what they should be experiencing.

Some people genuinely believe they can't meditate; they've tried it before and found it too difficult so they gave up. But everyone can meditate! It does require commitment and practice but to claim that we *can't* meditate is like saying we can't relax; everyone can relax, though they perhaps have never learned how. The secret of successful practice lies in establishing a regular opportunity each day to relax, with your attention placed singularly in the present moment of your awareness.

With each daily routine, your skill will improve and you will find, after a time, that the thoughts that keep popping into your mind begin to slow down and eventually stop completely. When you reach this stage, you have learned to simply 'be' in the present moment, free of the labels and judgmental thoughts we have learned to associate with ourselves and our experiences. In this state of mind, the problems of low self-esteem seem unimaginable.

The correct physical posture for meditation causes a lot of

confusion. The general perception is that we must sit cross-legged on the floor, which discourages many who find this uncomfortable. But it doesn't really matter how you sit or even if you sit at all. You can meditate while standing, walking, jogging, or lying flat on your back; in fact even while swimming! If you do sit cross-legged, sit on a cushion, as this elevates your seat to a position higher than your ankles. The most important thing is to be comfortable. Lying down is fine, though you may tend to fall asleep. If so, don't feel bad; it probably indicates that you needed a nap, so you provided your system with exactly what it needed at that time. Switching off phones, TV or anything else that may come crashing into your awareness is also a good idea.

Meditation does not come easily. A beautiful tree grows slowly.

One must wait for the blossom, the ripening of the fruit and the ultimate taste.

The blossom of meditation is an inexpressible peace that permeates the entire being.

Its fruit is ... indescribable.

Swami Vishnu Devananda

So how do we learn to *be* in meditation?

Every journey begins with the first step, and if we begin simply we'll be more likely to continue. The following simple meditation will provide the foundation for reaching a reasonable level of ability. Once you become familiar with it, you'll need no further guidance. You need only begin and then continue to practice at least once each day at your convenience and in your own time. Be assured that through your commitment and practice your insights will ripen and you will intuitively know exactly what to do next to take your practice to the next level.

Please read on to the end of this chapter before you try the following meditation.

Exercise: Mindfulness Meditation

Choose a suitable and safe place to meditate, preferably somewhere you don't normally spend lots of time. Also try to set aside a regular time and place that you will begin to associate with your practice. Your meditation will be more effective if you create the right setting, so remove any distractions and spend a few moments on centering.

Step 1: Becoming Centered

1. Make yourself comfortable in your chosen place and allow yourself to relax.
2. Continue to breathe normally and steadily; and when you are ready, close your eyes.
3. Place your internal attention on your breathing and follow each breath as it enters and leaves your body; notice if the incoming breath is slightly cooler than the outgoing one.
4. Imagine a flow of internal tension leaving your body each time you breathe out.
5. Imagine a beautiful and peaceful energy entering your body each time you breathe in.

Continue in this way, keeping your attention on the gentle flow of your breath as it comes and goes. If your thoughts drift on to something else, gently return them to your breathing.

Practice this centering exercise for at least two or three minutes before moving to Step 2. The more you practice this first step, the easier your meditation will become.

Step 2: Meditation

Begin again as in Step 1 with your eyes closed. Continue until you can easily hold your attention on your breath without the distraction of thoughts popping up.

Remember: you are not using this meditation to go somewhere else or enter a trance; you are using it to be fully present where you are, here and now.

Close your eyes and direct the focus of your attention internally.

As your thoughts arise, do not resist them; simply observe them and allow them to pass without becoming attached or involved.

Hold the focus of your attention here in the current moment as the silent observer.

Gently direct your attention to notice the subtle space between each new thought.

Continue in this way for at least five minutes or until you want to finish, though you should ideally try to continue for two minutes beyond that point, as this will help train your mind to focus for longer in future sessions.

This simple meditation is a valuable way to begin your practice since it acknowledges our inability to control the thoughts that pop into our mind and helps us become non-judgmental independent observers of them. The trick here is to simply observe what shows up without being carried away by it, as we might be aware of a flock of passing birds while keeping our attention focused on the distant horizon.

Daily practice for at least five minutes will quickly improve your ability and you'll soon find it easier to slip into a state of inner peace and tranquility. However, as with most things, there will be days when your mind is more active than usual, making your practice seem harder. If this happens, don't be frustrated; remember that having a mind which randomly wanders is part of being human. Simply return your attention to your breath, observing the in-and-out flow for a moment, before gently guiding it back to the stillness between your thoughts.

This simple meditation is designed to take you beyond fears and judgments, so be aware that any internal voice that suggests you might look silly or that you aren't doing it right is merely your ego mind trying to disrupt your efforts and keep you trapped in its illusions.

If the mind is not contrived it is spontaneously blissful, just as water, transparent and clear.
Tibetan saying

It can be helpful to reflect on something important before you begin, as if you were posing a question to yourself. Then simply release the question from your awareness and make no attempt to consciously search for an answer.

* * *

Some years ago, while on a visit to California, I was invited to join a group meditation taking place at the Chopra Center for Wellbeing in Carlsbad, La Jolla. The invitation seemed to arise by pure chance since I had no idea the session was taking place and had only arrived at the center a few minutes earlier. I was grateful to the universe for this unexpected opportunity to be included in this meditation and was particularly impressed by three questions the leaders asked at the start. Since the unconscious mind finds questions of any kind stimulating, I offer them here as they may prove useful to your practice:

1. What do I really want?
2. Who am I?
3. What is my life's purpose?

These are surely three of the most important questions we could ask ourselves. And there only one person who can ever provide an answer. You will notice, as your meditation skills develop, that you begin to see yourself and your world very differently as the answers to these and many other questions become clearer. This insightful shift in your awareness comes not from learning something new but by remembering how to reopen your mind to the nurturing energy of love. Our enlightenment lies in remembering what we may have forgotten: how to be kind to ourselves, our world, and all who share it with us.

You cannot do a kindness too soon because you never know how soon it will be too late.
Ralph Waldo Emerson

Another useful option you may wish to try is a mantra. A mantra is a sound or any word or phrase that you repeat during your meditation to help focus your mind. Mantras are used more frequently in Eastern cultures because it is believed certain sounds hold specific spiritual values. Mantras are less common in the West, possibly because some Westerners feel slightly self-conscious chanting a particular sound over and over again. However, if you'd like to use a mantra to help focus yourself, bear a couple of things in mind.

First, make the sound of your mantra on each out-breath as this enables you to breathe comfortably at the same time. Buddhist practitioners commonly use mantras that include the sounds 'Om', 'Hum', and 'Ah' because these are sounds which in traditional Tibetan culture represent spiritual connection, harmony and life.

Second, your mantra need not be a foreign word. Any sound is acceptable if it helps your meditation, such as the words 'relax', 'peace', and 'love'. The important thing is to establish an effortless, almost hypnotic cycle in which each sound you create seems to merge seamlessly into the fading resonance of its predecessor.

It's easy in our busy lives to put off until tomorrow what we need today. Your challenge now is to practice the simple meditation exercise in this chapter for at least two to three minutes each day. Once you can sit comfortably for that long, increase your meditation by a couple of minutes every few days until you can sit quite easily for 20 minutes. Doing this once a day will produce some amazing differences in the way you feel about everything, most importantly about yourself. The basic meditation given in this chapter is all you need to get started and you will instinctively know how to take the next step on your journey of mindfulness. Becoming skilled in meditation won't require intense concentration or lots of hard work; in fact it should require little effort. This really is a case of 'less is more'.

Competence comes from meditating little and often, as this internalizes your practice into an unconscious habit rather than a conscious daily chore. Habits are easy to set up and, once in place, require little effort to maintain, so try to turn your practice into a habit as quickly as possible. Two essential factors help our unconscious mind to achieve this:

1. Be consistent. Choose a regular time and place in which to practice. The more often you do something in the same way, the more quickly it is established as a pattern in your unconscious mind.
2. Learn how to overcome your 'can't be bothered' self-talk. This is the most common obstacle to any new behavior, such as attending a gym or a language class. We've all heard that internal voice telling us we can miss our practice today, that we can do double tomorrow. But this self-talk robs us of a valuable daily link and we must find a way to continue when it tells us to quit. Identify the circumstances that make it easy for you to meditate and those that make it more difficult, then adjust your routines accordingly.

Regular practice of meditation will create cumulative positive effects in your sense of self and general well-being. At the end of his long life, the Buddha offered his followers this advice in pursuit of their own enlightenment: 'Be a light unto yourself.' Possibly they were expecting to hear much more from him, yet perhaps we can understand what he meant. Perhaps he was trying to explain that they already had everything they would need to create greater happiness in their lives; they only needed to rediscover it.

Seeking happiness outside of ourselves is like waiting for sunshine in a cave facing north.
Tibetan saying

Let each meditation move you one step closer to your true self and gently reawaken a new awareness of your world and the part you will play in it. In mindfulness meditation, we have gained yet another valuable key to unconscious confidence and higher self-esteem, though we have not yet reached the end of our journey.

As our technical and scientific understanding becomes more advanced, it seems our awareness of self is getting smaller. Meditation may seem an unexpected way to create unconscious self-esteem, but it is effective because it involves an improvement in our understanding of self. It confirms beyond doubt in these times of shrinking spirituality that we are already perfect at our source and don't need to be fixed in any way. Meditation nurtures an understanding of your true self and empowers a clearer sense of purpose. One of the deepest desires of the human mind is the desire for meaning, yet it seems we must come full circle to find the answers, for what we seek is already known to us and we need only realize who we really are in order to remember it.

Meditation is not religion yet it certainly is a spiritual practice, for it aligns the human mind with the passenger spirit within. The word 'spirituality' is merely a label our culture uses in an attempt to describe our true self, therefore no course that seeks to improve self-esteem is complete without some understanding of spirituality. In mindfulness meditation we awaken to the simple reality that we are much more than the sum of our mind, or the person we've been led to believe we are. At last we begin to understand the true source of unconscious self-esteem.

Quick Start: Resources
Breath awareness exercise
When used properly, this calming exercise should be easy and comfortable to practice daily. Try to develop a regular slot of my time in which to nourish and connect with yourself.

Close your eyes.

Place your attention on your breathing.

1. Silently count the seconds that pass as you inhale gently through your nose.
2. Hold the breath at the top of your inhalation for a silent count of two seconds.
3. Breathe out through your mouth for twice as long as it took to breathe in.

The trick here is to breathe out for a count that is double what you took to breathe in. For example, if you inhaled to a count of 3, then you would hold it for two seconds, and then breathe out to a count of 6.

You need only do this for about two or three minutes in order to notice a big difference.

It's extremely important here to *breathe in through your nose* and *out through your mouth*.

This simple breathing technique will create a calming energy in any situation or place. Those who become stressed while shopping need only find a shop window to stare into while practicing this technique; passers-by will simply assume you are window shopping!

10

All You Need is Love

Some day, after we have mastered the winds, the waves, the tides and gravity, we will harness the energies of love. Then, for a second time in the history of the world man will have discovered fire.
Pierre Teilhard de Chardin

There's a story attributed to Dan Millman, author of *The Way of the Peaceful Warrior*, which tells of a young girl named Sashi. Soon after Sashi's baby brother was born, she began asking her parents if she could spend some time alone with the baby. At first they refused, fearing Sashi might be jealous of her new brother, but her requests became increasingly persistent and finally they agreed. After all, she had never shown signs of jealousy and her parents knew her to be a kind and sensitive girl. Delighted at this news, Sashi immediately went into the baby's room and almost closed the door behind her, though it remained open just a few inches so her parents could listen in and watch what was happening.

What they saw and heard amazed them.

Sashi walked over to her brother's crib and placed her face very close to his. Then, in a soft voice, she whispered, 'Baby, tell me what God feels like. I'm afraid I'm starting to forget.'

We live in a time when the spiritual fabric of our world seems to be unraveling before our eyes, causing many to feel separated from their true sense of self and purpose. Yet this is an age when we need more than ever to access our deeper sense of spirituality if we hope to move forward in peace, and we can only do that by looking within. There is an energy in each of us which transcends the boundaries of our limited perceptual awareness, a healing energy that restores and nourishes us when we need it most. This is no physical aspect of our being, therefore it can't be quantified. We are so much more than what we see in the mirror, more than our transitory moods or behaviors and beliefs. Too often, we limit ourselves by confining our sense of self within these petty illusions of identity and separation whereas in reality we are timeless and boundless. We are not separate from everything else; we don't just live 'in' nature – we are a fundamental part of it. We are, in essence, the pure energy of the universe.

The Sioux idea of living creatures is that trees, buffalo and man are temporary energy swirls, and turbulent patterns ... We find this perception registered so many ways in archaic and primitive lore. I say that it is probably the most basic insight into the nature of things, and that our more common, recent occidental view of the universe as consisting of fixed things is out of the mainstream, a deviation from basic human perception.
Gary Snyder

As we begin to realize who we really are, it becomes clear that we live in a universe of endless possibilities. There is an energy that exists throughout the entire universe from the smallest molecule to the furthest outskirts of the cosmos. It is everywhere and in everything, which means there can be no place where it is not, including ourselves. Up to now, we've focused on rewriting the programs of our unconscious mind, but we also have access to a far greater resource for change than the functions of our mind. Our mind and all its abilities, both conscious and unconscious, can never be more than a dimension of our body, so it is a critical mistake to identify ourselves as our mind – this is like identifying yourself as your leg or elbow. Clearly, the mind and body are both parts of the same system, but it's extremely important to our sense of identity to remember that our body more accurately represents where we are than who we are.

We are much more than the sum of our physical parts; we are

in essence energy manifesting in physical form. In this final chapter we will explore the relationship between your mind, the voice you hear there, and the energy that is your true self. We will consider who we really are beyond the self-perpetuating illusions of the ego mind and discover what happens if we step out of this illusion even for a few brief moments. As we look at the mass of particles staring back at us from the mirror, we shall soon realize how invaluable is the capacity to look beneath the surface of this 'pool'.

There are no empty spaces on this planet. What seems to us like empty space is in fact a combination of carbon, hydrogen, oxygen, nitrogen, and a few other ingredients necessary for us to breathe. The illusion of emptiness and solid structures in our universe is created by our limited capacity to see things as they really are, including at the subatomic and quantum level. You may look in the mirror and believe what you see there is a solid physical mass, yet if we could condense together the solid mass of every person in the world the result would be roughly the same size as a sugar cube. What appears to be solid matter – for example, a table – seems to be so only because we can't see it from a subatomic perspective; a physicist would tell us that the table at a quantum level of awareness is really a field of energy, and that energy consists primarily of 99.9% empty space.

> *If grass can grow through cement, love can find you at every time in your life.*
> Cher

While no one really understands quantum theory, we do know that particles vibrate at different levels and that energy on a certain level will attract similar energy. We also know that thoughts are a form of energy that finds physical expression in the universe – another reason to be fussy what we think about, for the energy generated will attract similar energies back into our life. The idea that our thoughts find physical expression can be demonstrated scientifically since the physical aspect of our world is matter, and matter at a quantum level is made up of particles of energy.

In 1965 the Nobel Prize for Physics was awarded to the American scientist Richard Feynman, who was gaining prominence for his innovative work in the field of particle physics. His early development had been favorably compared to that of Albert Einstein, so it's safe to assume that Feynman knew his subatomic particles from his waves; yet even he conceded that no one fully understood how quantum theory works, famously remarking that 'anyone who claims to understand quantum theory doesn't understand quantum theory'. Happily, thanks to people like Einstein and Feynman, we don't have to understand how it works; we need only appreciate how powerfully these universal laws influence our existence.

If we could experience our world from a quantum level of perception, we would see an infinite field of continuously changing energy. This is interpreted by the eye of an observer as a solid mass, yet Einstein's famous equation $E = mc^2$ tells us this is an illusion – it cannot be true. If we accept that energy (E) equals mass squared (m^2), we must conclude that one equals the other squared, therefore mass and energy must be the same. The moment we first realize this, we begin to see ourselves differently. We stop identifying ourselves as the swirling mass of transitory molecules we see in the mirror and realize that what we see there is an infinite and ever-changing field of energy and information that we have mistakenly labeled 'me'.

At our level of perception the tissue and fiber we see reflected in the mirror seem to provide a fairly accurate description of who we are, but in this we are greatly deceived since there is not a single cell present in our body today that was there two years ago. The word 'cell' comes from a Latin word meaning 'small room', and every life form on this planet is made up of them –

they are literally the building blocks of life. Humans are multicellular life forms; we each consist of around 100 trillion cells of intelligence and information, apparently solid but in fact 99.9% empty space. This might present those who believe *they are* their physical body with something of an identity crisis. Is it possible that we are not what we see in the mirror, that we are simply the observer of what we see there?

At the heart of each of us, whatever our imperfections, there exists a silent pulse of perfect rhythm, a complex of wave forms and resonances, which is absolutely individual and unique, and yet which connects us to everything in the Universe.
George Leonard

We see the energy and intelligence of life everywhere. We see it moving at lightning speeds in the amazing spectacle of a large flock of starlings in aerial synchronization, soaring and plunging as one through an early evening sky, and wonder how so many pairs of wings can elegantly and seamlessly choreograph this awesome spectacle without a single collision. Shoals of fish move as one body, turning in perfect synchronization, seemingly without any detectable means of communication between the first and last fish, yet each fish seems to be tuned into an invisible energy of collective communication. Every culture in history has found its own unique way to describe the all-permeating energy of life. In Japan it is known as ki, hence the term reiki, a powerful form of energy healing that reduces stress and promotes well-being. In China, tai chi practitioners call this energy chi, understanding the essential relationship between energy and movement – as do those who practice the ancient art of feng shui to harmoniously redirect the flow of energy through homes and workplaces. In Hebrew, this energy is ruach, meaning 'Holy Spirit', while the ancient cultures of the Indian continent call it prana, a Sanskrit word meaning 'vital force'. While each culture uses a different label to describe it, all agree that the essence of our true self is energy and that the way to restore good health and well-being lies in creating harmony and balance in our personal energy.

Since our true nature is both timeless and boundless, we can't be confined by the labels of our emotions and behaviors and we can never totally disconnect from who we are. There may be times as we journey through life when we feel totally disconnected from our higher self, yet in reality this is impossible to do: what we perceive as separation is merely an illusion created by the trance of material and external referral. We can choose to identify our self with anything from a mood to a behavior, and we can keep that illusion in place throughout our life, letting our ego mind create a sense of self-fuelled fear. Or we can remember who we really are and begin living our lives on purpose.

Even when we feel most alone, in reality we can never disconnect from our true energy source; we can only disconnect from our awareness of it, which is not the same thing at all. As the song says, 'You can check out anytime you like, but you can never leave.'

Since energy is in everything, including our emotions, we must understand that we can only truly change our lives by understanding how to change the type of energy that flows into our life. Happily, the energy of life is everywhere, which means we don't need to do much more than cultivate a different awareness of it. Water, especially in its natural form as a river, lake or ocean, is a great source of energy or *chi*. Earth too can offer us abundant energy that nourishes us at every level. We can tap into this energy very easily simply by *being* present with it in the moment. We don't have to do much at all, except choose to be still and mindful of our surroundings. We only need to stand barefoot on cool grass with a relaxed and peaceful mind for a few moments to sense the energy in the ground; or place our hands or feet along with our attention into a river for a few seconds to become aware of the powerful energy in the water. In that brief moment of interaction we reconnect to an energy that restores and nourishes us, as it flows with harmony and peace through our entire being.

Life was never meant to be a struggle, just a gentle progression from one point to another, much like walking through a valley on a sunny day.
Stuart Wilde, *Affirmations*

Many people believe they would struggle to find time in their busy life to simply *be* with the energy that surrounds them. They say it isn't realistic to think we can reconnect with nature among the concrete and steel of a bustling city, yet even in the midst of our biggest cosmopolitan centers there are opportunities to reconnect with the energy of life in its most natural state. Almost every town and city has at least one public park where you can take off your shoes and socks, stand on the grass, and sense the natural energy in the ground beneath your feet even for a few minutes. Standing barefoot on the earth is something very few adults do enough of, yet as children we couldn't shed our shoes and socks fast enough and when we revisit the habit we quickly remember why. The moment we stand barefoot on the grass we feel just a little less stressed, it becomes harder to be serious or to worry, we sense something very natural is happening, and a primordial awareness begins to stir. Understandably, we might feel less inclined to do this in the depths of a freezing winter but we could walk through a park in the crisp air, focusing our attention on the energy of our natural surroundings.

In the same way, when you sit near a river and place your attention on its steadily moving waters, you become more mindful of the energy connection that exists between you and the river. If the water is reasonably clean, you can place your hands in it; as you sense its energy flowing effortlessly through your fingers, bring your attention to your hands and breathe, gently aware that you and the water share the same restorative energy of life. Our natural ability to nurture this connection can be accessed at any time as long as we are mindful that greater happiness lies not in the path we follow but in the heart and mind of the one who walks it.

What lies behind us and what lies before us are tiny matters compared to what lies within us.
Ralph Waldo Emerson

High self-esteem is the unconscious legacy of our ability to place our conscious awareness on the energy of love and to discover it not only in ourselves but in everything. The energy we hold in our body and mind continuously finds expression in our lives, and we will find it difficult to feel genuinely happy with ourselves while holding judgmental or angry thoughts about others. Thoughts are energy and it's a proven scientific fact that energy of every kind attracts anything that vibrates at a similar frequency to itself, therefore if we desire more peace in our lives, we must be the peace we desire, because if we try to adopt an air of peace while holding the energy of anger, we'll produce only an aggressive-looking peace activist. Self-esteem is founded on love, not anger. If we hope to generate more of it in our lives we must start looking for it in others and this becomes so much easier to do when we change the way we see things, including ourselves.

Change your preconceived notions of how things are for just a few minutes each day and allow yourself to see everything as a form of energy. It's been said that we are spiritual beings having a temporary human experience rather than the other way around; it follows from this that no one is who we see, since all we see is human form. Seeing things differently, even for a few seconds, creates an insightful perceptual shift. You will find the energy of love everywhere. Do not be fooled by the fearful or angry faces you pass in the street; the mask they show you is not who they are but merely a reflection of their current state of mind.

Every day on the streets I see the face of Jesus, in its many wonderful disguises.
Mother Teresa

Try seeing people differently on your way to work or any place where you are with others. Develop compassion of perception and search for the kindness hidden behind their masks. Every one of those faces belongs to a person tied to you by at least one thing: they want to be happy and they're pursuing happiness by following a path they believe will take them there. That path may have led them into some dark and fearful places, and when you see them, they may be out of balance with their true self and completely unaware of the healing energy that lies within them. Those faces are only reflections in the pool of life, and if we have the wisdom to look beneath the surface we will find an energy which connects everyone and everything in the universe.

Award-winning journalist Lynne McTaggart explains in her excellent book, *The Field: The Quest for the Secret Force of the Universe,* that we're all connected to each other at a level beyond that of visual perception: 'At our most elemental we are not a chemical reaction but an energetic charge. Human beings and all living things are a coalescence of energy in a field of energy, connected to every other thing in the world.'

Greater happiness is created by directing the energy of love towards ourselves and others. Love of self, love of life, and love of others awakens an energy that lifts us above the fears and limitations of our negative thoughts. The energy of love connects us all, and when we start to look for it in the world around us we discover an abundance of it within ourselves.

Love is within you. It's always been there, and reawakening

your awareness of it is the kindest gift you could give yourself.

Some people say they don't know how to love themselves – which is like saying they don't know how to smile or laugh. In either case you can choose whether you will or you won't, but you can never say that you don't know how to. The energy of love is an essential aspect of healing and recovery in all cases of emotional trauma. Successful psychotherapy rests on re-establishing and strengthening the energy of love towards our self. In fact 'psychotherapy' is a combination of two words, *psych-* meaning 'spirit' and *therapy* meaning 'to nurse'; thus when people help themselves in this way, they are literally 'nursing their spirit'.

Psychoanalysis is in essence a cure through love.
Sigmund Freud

Self-esteem flows effortlessly from the energy of love which is exactly who you are at source, and raising your awareness of your true self generates this flow of unconscious self-esteem into every part of your life.

How can we start doing this now?

We do it by reopening our awareness of the energy around and within us, and committing to look for and sense it in at least *one* experience each day. It may be something in nature, in the face or behavior of another, or perhaps something you notice about yourself. You can begin right now by gently placing your awareness on yourself here in this present moment. Right now is the only time you will ever have, so use it wisely; sense the subtle presence of universal energy which permeates everywhere and everything. You can spend your time in thoughts about tomorrow or yesterday, but both are merely illusions of the mind and have no existence outside it. The present moment is different. It's real and it's here, and it's the only place that will ever exist. All our past- or future-based thinking can only ever exist here in the present. Therefore now is where we must place our attention.

Exercise

1. Make the time at least once a day to lift the veil of sensory-based illusion for five minutes.
2. Sit quietly and sense the gifts the present moment brings into your life.
3. Can you sense the energy in the air, the sky, or the presence of the people around you?
4. Ignore the ego mind as it tries to distract you away with past- or future-based thoughts.
5. Observe everything in this moment from the peaceful perspective of a silent witness.

We travel life's pathway in the energy of love; we are free to acknowledge or ignore it as we choose, though it remains within regardless of the choices we make. This is the energy of the universe, and whether you are aware of it or not, the simple truth is that you are now and always will be *in* love, literally!

The most overlooked resource we have is our ability to direct and receive love. It's an essential aspect of our true nature and exists in each of us in abundance. It is something we can never run out of – we can only close down our awareness of it. Sadly we tend to do exactly that at the times in our life when we need it most. It is now widely acknowledged that our immune system can be greatly influenced by feelings of love or compassion for ourselves and others. Research has found that powerful hormonal and biological changes occur when we experience certain feelings such as intense happiness or deep spirituality; these increase the secretion of hormones such as serotonin, dopamine, and other immune modulators. Serotonin is an important hormone that influences our mood, sleep patterns, metabolic rate, appetite etc. Studies show that animals with low levels of serotonin demonstrate much higher levels of aggression, and people who are in a state of intense stress quickly calm down when their serotonin levels are increased.

Many synthetic anti-depressants contain serotonin, even though we can all produce it naturally when we feel intense joy or love. If, at least once a day, you can sense the connecting energy of love in your life, or spend a few moments in quiet reflection of the present moment, or laugh just a little more, the healthy beneficial effect on your emotions and immune system will come from a natural rather than synthetic source.

If I told patients to raise their blood levels of immune globulins or killer T-cells to heal themselves no one would know how. But if I can teach them to love themselves and others fully, the exact same change happens automatically.

The truth is: Love heals.

Bernie Siegel

If we believe we are spiritual beings at our source (and every religion holds this to be true), then within each of us lies the potential to achieve far more than we might currently realize. We tend to associate our true self with our mind, yet we can't escape the fact that the mind is just another aspect of our body. What about the unconscious mind – could that be who we really are? Absolutely not. The unconscious mind is merely a metaphor or label we use to describe the internal activity of the mind that we are not consciously aware of. Whilst it can provide a rich and amazing resource for change, it remains just another aspect of our physical body. If we are truly spiritual energy in essence, we can never be our physical body, behavior, or state of mind – anymore than we are the car we drive or the clothes we wear. These are useful aspects of our lives but they're not who we are and they never will be; they are merely the material ingredients in the journey we call life.

It can be easy to fall further into the illusion that we are what we see in the mirror. We may even believe we have little choice in the matter of how we see ourselves, but we do have a choice, and it begins by choosing to see through new eyes. We need only scratch the surface of the physical manifestation we have learned to identify as 'me' to discover who we really are and see what we may yet become.

Story

There's an ancient temple in Thailand called the Temple of the Golden Buddha. It contains an eight-foot-tall solid gold statue of the Buddha, which is about 750 years old and extremely valuable. Around 500 years ago the Burmese army invaded Thailand, looting and pillaging as they went. The priests in charge of the temple knew the invading army was coming their way and realized that as soon as the invaders saw this eight-foot solid gold statue they would carry it off, so in order to protect it they covered it entirely with clay. They did an excellent job, and when the invaders arrived and entered the temple, all they saw was a simple clay statue.

Unfortunately the plan backfired slightly. Because they couldn't find any gold, the soldiers got angry and killed everyone in the village, leaving no one alive who knew what was inside the statue.

There it remained for the next 500 years, without anyone ever suspecting what lay beneath the surface of the clay. In World War II, enemy soldiers came into the temple and saw the statue, but all the time the doors of the temple remained open and unguarded – for who would steal a worthless clay image?

Some years ago, the government decided to build a new road, and to do so the village temple would have to be moved and relocated elsewhere. When it came time to dismantle the building and transport any valuable items to the new site, the clay statue was included as it had high spiritual value.

The problem arose when people tried to lift it. It seemed to be fastened to the concrete base on which it rested, so, in an effort to keep it safe, they decided to dig around the base and lift it all with the help of heavy lifting equipment, as you might lift a root ball along with the plant.

As they lowered the statue onto the back of a truck, they thought they heard a crack and became alarmed that the sculpture might have been damaged. But due to the late hour they decided to leave the statue on the truck and assess the situation in the morning. So they threw a sheet over it and went home.

During the night it began to rain very hard and the priest in charge of the operation began to worry that the rain might affect the clay, so he went out with a flashlight to examine the statue.

As he lifted the sheet and shone his light into the darkness, he saw a golden light flash back at him and almost dropped his torch. Climbing onto the truck, he positioned the flashlight, took out his penknife, and began to scratch at the surface of the statue. As he scratched, the gold light grew in size until eventually, several hours later in the cold grey dawn, he found himself sitting face to face with an eight-foot-tall solid gold statue of the Buddha.

* * *

If you will scratch, just a little, at the surface of the person you have been *led to believe* you are, you will find an ocean of golden potential lying very close to the surface. However, there's only one person who can do that in your life and it's you.

Who else could it be? Who else would you want it to be?

You have always known you are much more than the illusion of the ego mind; beneath its deception there's always been an awareness that you are more than you allow yourself to see. Peel away this illusion you have learned to identify as yourself and welcome back an energy that has always been there with you, at every step of your journey, but has been absent from your awareness for much too long.

The time will come
when, with elation,
you will greet yourself arriving
at your own door, in your own mirror,
and each will smile at the other's welcome,

And say, sit here. Eat.
You will love again the stranger who was yourself.
Give wine. Give bread. Give back your heart
to itself, to the stranger who has loved you

all your life, whom you ignored
for another, who knows you by heart.
Take down the love letters from the bookshelf,

the photographs, the desperate notes,
peel your own image from the mirror.
Sit. Feast on your life.

Derek Walcott, 'Love after Love'

Think for a moment how many species of life exist on this beautiful planet, in the oceans and on the land. The entire planet is teeming with life. It's amazing to think how many different species share this world with us, yet despite this rich and complex diversity of life there is only one species that can contemplate its own existence or wonder at the mysteries of the universe. No other life form on this planet can sit and consider the possibilities that may exist beyond the outer regions of our solar system.

Is this unique ability merely the product of Darwinian chance?

Should we accept the idea that we are no more than the result of extreme coincidence, despite the fact that among the billions of other life forms not one has succumbed to anything approaching the same coincidence of evolutionary development? Or can we believe that the energy that sets us aside from every other life form on this planet cannot be quantified or measured by instruments and will depart when the physical frame it occupies is finally no more?

Who are we beyond the illusions of our subjective perception?

Who is the energy within you that is contemplating these questions now?

It isn't your mind, because sometimes your mind tells you to do something and another part of you overrules it. So who, we may ask, intervenes and overrules the mind's instructions?

However much uncertainty you may have in relation to these questions, there is one thing about which you can feel certainty: you are here in the journey of life for a reason. Perhaps you are here to share your talents and gifts; perhaps there's something you need to learn or do; maybe you are here for the simplest reason of all: you chose to be here because you thought it might be enjoyable and interesting.

Is it interesting, and how enjoyable have you allowed it to be thus far?

I hope that you will take at least one thing from these pages and use it to make your life much more interesting and enjoyable, for in doing that you will gain more than unconscious confidence and self-esteem; you will gain a new awareness of yourself and the unique gifts you have brought with you. Our journey together was born of a desire to create greater happiness by rewriting the programs of our unconscious mind, and our search has led us through a number of effective exercises and skills that are designed to create that outcome. But much has passed since we began and your desires may have changed now, along with your perception of self. The ability to create and sustain unconscious high self-esteem is useful, to say the least, but is it a new skill to be acquired by you or a natural ability you've learned to ignore?

Love is a fruit in season at all times, and within reach of every hand.
Mother Teresa of Calcutta

High self-esteem is merely a label which describes your ability to cultivate and sustain a healthy and natural love for yourself. As we've seen, love is the one thing which has always been in you from the start; it's there because *it is* you and you should no more feel uncomfortable in this energy than a fish would feel in water. To *be in love* with yourself is neither unnatural nor conceited; in fact since love is your true nature at source, it would be unnatural to do anything else. The illusion of self which has been created by the ego mind is an entirely unnatural and false representation of who you really are, and learning to improve your opinion of it will only be useful if you remain seduced by the illusion that you are your behavior, your moods, or the physical body you see in the mirror.

Self-realization breaks the spell of the ego mind through an awareness that you're already complete and do not need to be fixed, that you are where you are meant to be right now in your journey, and that you and the universe are well and truly on purpose.

We shall not cease from exploration
And the end of all our exploring
Will be to arrive where we started
And know the place for the first time.
T. S. Eliot

It may be that unconscious self-esteem is only what we believe we need most. It is possible that what we really need is an authentic awareness of our true nature and self, for in that valuable insight lies the potential for every unconscious change we could desire. In the days and weeks that lie ahead, you will have many opportunities to think differently.

It is my sincere hope that you have already begun to weave the strands of change from each chapter into a new awareness of yourself and your world. Greater happiness begins when we realize that the energy of love surrounds us in every moment. We can choose to fill our lives with it by training our unconscious mind to search for it in every experience, or we can choose to ignore it.

As a new awareness of self begins to unfold, we gain a precious gift in the knowledge that love is all we will ever need in order to feel happy and fulfilled, and that we carry an infinite supply of it. We don't need to persuade others to give us their love. All we need to do is give it away at every opportunity, and it will effortlessly appear in our lives, flooding back to us in abundance.

When all your desires are distilled
You will cast just two votes:
To love more
And to be happy.
Hafiz

May you embrace love, laughter, harmony and peace at each step of your journey.

Travel safely in the boundless energy of the Universe.
Namaste

References and Resources

Allen, James (1999) *As a Man Thinketh*, De Vorss & Company.

Castaneda, Carlos (1970) *The Teachings of Don Juan*, Penguin Books.

Chopra, Deepak (1994) *The Seven Spiritual Laws of Success*, Bantam Press.

Chopra Deepak (2003) *The Spontaneous Fulfillment of Desire*, Crown Publishing.

Chopra, Deepak (2003) *Synchrodestiny*, Crown Publishing, Random House.

Dyer, Wayne (1998) *Manifest Your Destiny*, Thorsons (Harper Collins).

Dyer, Wayne (2004) *The Power of Intention*, Hay House.

Frankl, Viktor (1997) *Man's Search for Meaning*, Simon & Schuster.

Garfield, Charles (1986) *Peak Performers*, William Morrow & Co.

Gawain, Shakti (2002) *Creative Visualization*, New World Library.

Gladwell, Malcolm (2005) *Blink*, Penguin Books.

James, William (1957) *The Principles of Psychology*, Dover Publications.

Jung, Carl (1991) *The Archetypes and the Collective Unconscious*, Routledge.

Jung, Carl (2001) *Modern Man in Search of a Soul*, Routledge.

Langer, Ellen J. (1990) *Mindfulness: Choice and Control in Everyday Life*, Da Capo Press.

Levey, Joel and Michelle (1998) *Living in Balance*, Conari Press.

McTaggart, Lynne (2001) *The Field*, HarperCollins.

McTaggart, Lynne (2008) *The Intention Experiment*, Harper Element.

Millman, Dan (1985) *The Way of the Peaceful Warrior*, H. J. Kramer.

Murphy, Joseph (2006) *The Power of Your Subconscious Mind*, Pocket Books.

Nuernberger, Phil (1996) *The Quest for Personal Power*, The

Berkley Publishing Group.

O'Connor, Joseph and Seymour, John (1990) *Introducing NLP*, Thorsons (HarperCollins).

O'Hanlon, Bill (1987) *Taproots*, W. W. Norton & Co.

O'Hanlon, Bill (1992) *Solution-Oriented Hypnosis*, W. W. Norton & Co.

Rose Charvet, Shelle (1997) *Words that Change Minds*, Kendall/ Hunt Publishing Co.

Rosen, Sidney (1991) *The Teaching Tales of Milton H. Erickson*, W. W. Norton & Co.

Ruiz, Miguel (1997) *The Four Agreements*, Amber Allen Publishing.

Tolle, Eckhart (2001) *The Power of Now*, Mobius Publishing.

Walcott, Derek (1986) *Collected Poems 1948–84*, Farrar, Straus & Giroux.

Williamson, Marianne (1996) *A Return To Love*, Harper.

About the Author

Gary Dooley is a facilitator and founder of the Life Balance Personal Development Course.

A master practitioner of Neuro-Linguistic Programming, he has lived in Canada where his family originates and now lives in Lancashire, England.

BOOKS

O is a symbol of the world, of oneness and unity. In different cultures it also means the "eye," symbolizing knowledge and insight. We aim to publish books that are accessible, constructive and that challenge accepted opinion, both that of academia and the "moral majority."

Our books are available in all good English language bookstores worldwide. If you don't see the book on the shelves ask the bookstore to order it for you, quoting the ISBN number and title. Alternatively you can order online (all major online retail sites carry our titles) or contact the distributor in the relevant country, listed on the copyright page.

See our website www.o-books.net for a full list of over 500 titles, growing by 100 a year.

And tune in to myspiritradio.com for our book review radio show, hosted by June-Elleni Laine, where you can listen to the authors discussing their books.

MySpiritRadio